KNOW THYSELF

(स्वयंसिद्धा)

KRISHAN ANEJA

ISBN 979-8-88641-549-0

Welcome, my esteemed readers!

Beg to be excused to say I am no Guru of any shade. Go through 'Know Thyself' and determine for yourself whether it offers ideas relevant to sailing through life smoothly. The discussions herein are a summary of practical inputs picked up by me in my eventful journey.

Your frank views are welcome.

Email- aneja.krishanlal@gmail.com

DEDICATED TO,

I. My Father, late Shri M R Aneja(1900-1939)

(Matriculate, (1920-22) Punjab University, Lahore)

A man of solemn emulative principles, dignified behavior style, high integrity and uncompromising self-esteem that he was, inspired confidence while handling affairs of life. Praiseworthy behavior, free interactive style and conduct were his forte.

Quite often, my mother, when a bit free from the burden of house-hold chores, would sit down and bring up before us how he used to handle the affairs of life with determination, open mind, passion, honesty of purpose and fairness with malice to none.

Alas, cruel destiny snatched him away at a young age. God be merciful!

II. My life-partner, Krishna Aneja

A loving mother singularly committed to welfare of her progeny that she is, willingly and happily, puts behind all other considerations when growth, happiness and future of children demands so.

A God fearing, deeply religious individual with total faith in HIM is her forte. She firmly believes that singing devotional songs in HIS Praise with 'Shradha' is as essential as taking care of one's other daily routines.

Uncompromising efforts and dedication for the family's interests are supreme for her even if it means neglecting herself and others. A firm decision taken after due process of churning must be put to test to ensure its successful culmination into success.

CONTENTS

Contents

Distinguished Fellow, **USI,** *New Delhi*
Fellow, **Royal Asiatic Society of Great Britain and Ireland**
Honorary Research Affiliate, **LMFSAI,** *Harvard University*
Festival Director, **Valley of Words** *International Literature & Arts Festival, Dehradun*

Dr. Sanjeev Chopra Historian, Policy Analyst & Columnist

FOREWORD

Cogito Ergo Sum: *I think, therefore I am*
> Rene Descartes (1637)

Know then Thyself,
Presume not God to scan,
The proper study of mankind is Man
> Alexander Pope (1720)

KL Aneja's short treatise **Know Thyself** on life, success, professional growth, work-life balance and the joys of 'second innings' is replete with anecdotes, quotes of wise men and an attitude that brims with hope and positivity. Before I discuss this offering, I would like to mention that his autobiography **Karmath Jeevan** is a very valuable addition to the oeuvre of partition literature. While poets, story tellers, novelists, historians, thespians, and film makers have all given their take on the partition, Aneja has written his matter-of-fact story to show how adversity can be overcome by sheer hard work, mentorship of seniors, and of course bychoosing 'the time when the tides are high'! The crystallised wisdom based on the experiences of his personal life have been brought together in this book in which he takes up myriad themes: success, professional knowledge and competence, self-appraisal and finally the joys and blues of retirement.

Aneja says that as human beings are the apex of creation, they have an opportunity as well as a responsibility for achieving excellence. Only a human being can aspire to be a Karam Yogi: in fact, he argues that the best a human being can do is to focus on his/her action with complete devotion and dedication, irrespective of the result, for as the Geeta says – work is the only variable over which a human being has some degree of control – for we do not chose our teams or the circumstances into which we are thrust. Aneja, and lakhs like him were in the turmoil of Partition for no fault of theirs–that was 'fate'– but some like Aneja worked to create their own 'destiny'. For even though there was economic deprivation, his mother gave him invaluable 'sanskars'. He learnt to introspectand strivefor perfection. From an early age,he understood the significance of Prayer and was firm in his commitment to Truth. Aneja makes it a point to mention that while it is important to be a good speaker, it is even more importantto be a good listener and a keen observer. These are important life skills which supplement the professional and domain skills that every professional needs to acquire (in Aneja's case – accounting).

Anejas advise to all youngwomen and men is that every morn is the dawn of a new hope and endless opportunities. Obviously, he is a member of the 5 am club, and recommends a life in which punctuality and orderliness play asignificant role.

What I have like most in this book is the concept of success. He explains that 'success is not a tangible commodity': it is more to do with the inner urge to achieve 'whatever is valuable'. But success does not come about by itself – one must work on it with commitment, zeal, and honesty of purpose. If one wants to achieve something, or for that matter anything in life, one will have to immerse oneself fully in the cause.

"Mita de apni hasti ko agar kutch martaba chahiye.
ke dana khak mein mil kar gule gulzar hota hai."

("Finish your ego, care not for self if you want to achieve something! Just as aseed merge in the earth before mesmerising the garden with its flowering")

While we must celebrate our success,one should not gloat over it, or be carried away with it. Aneja explains that there is a fine balance between 'success' and 'unscrupulous ambition'. He also warns us against another fallout of success:arrogance. 'Arrogance shoots up from no-where just after the first signs of success and is followed by the tendency to be intolerant, followed by the big brother, greed. While a discerning ambitious person may be well-aware of not letting the success go to one's head there is an imminent possibility of arrogance, ill behaviour, and greed lurking in the shadows. Likewise, unscrupulous ambition makes one believe that one is always right and has asuperior place in society, thus making him immune to scrutiny and criticism.This to Aneja is the beginning of the end.

What then is the answer to this conundrum? Perhaps, Mahatma Gandhi's vision of Trusteeship is the real answer. You hold your wealth and estate as an 'amanat' (to be carried forward to the next generation for public good), rather than as a 'jagir' (private estate for private profit). Only Trusteeship can bring contentment (Trupti in Hindi) which is most sacrosanct idiom of a blissful and satisfied life.

In fine, ***Know Thyself*** is an eminently readable book which you must have on your bookshelf. It will help you elevate your thoughts and feeling when you are feeling low, and it will help you find the right quotes for the right occasions besides giving you the wisdom and equanimity to understand that finally one must be prepared for retirement as well as the journey beyond this life. I will end by this meaningful quote from Buddha: your purpose in life is to find yourpurpose and give your heart and soul to it'. Aneja's life is an exemplar: he defined success, worked towards it, maintained a life work balance and is now giving back to the society all that he has learnt from the opportunities and adversities that came his way. You are born into the eco system of fate – but you can carve out your destiny if you 'know thyself!'

Sanjeev Chopra

Phone: +91 1352608722 Email: choprasanjeev@gamil.com; sanjeevchopra@fas.harvard.edu 43 USHA, Sahastradhara Road, Dehradun 248013 Uttarakhand INDIA www.valleyofwords.org

KNOW THYSELF IS A TREATISE ON LIFE

REVIEWS

After his debut book KARMATH JEEVAN in 2015, Krishan Aneja has now come out with a thought-provoking treatise 'KNOW THY SELF'. It is truly amazing that a retired senior government-ONGC officer should, in the octogenarian decade of his life, feel inspired to bring up a treatise on how to shape and conduct the affairs of lifein its totality with serene satisfaction, grace and commendable success.

His KARMATH JEEVAN had primarily focused on the journey of his own life. As an 11-year old migrant from Pakistan, he had spent quite a few months in a refugee camp. Thereafter, he managed to duly graduate. His first job was in the Audit and Accounts Department, Shimla. Over the following few years, he changed jobs and eventually superannuated in 1994 as a general manager in ONGC.

KNOW THY SELF, as its title suggests, tells the reader to go on a journey of *self-discovery*. Even though professional success is much cherished, it alone cannot be the final milestone in one's life journey; one must also learn to be a worldly wise and street smart individual.

The Book is divided into four parts. The first Part discusses in-depth the nuances of a balanced and rewarding life, and takes a deep peep into the important facets of life. The Part II dwells on such topics that are meant to serve as add-ons to one's professional knowledge and competence. The Part III involves *"brain storming for self appraisal"* and defines the various stages in life, and how to make those easy and stress free. And finally, Part IV covers miscellaneous topics such as the issues and the anxieties associated with post-retirement life.

The author's life experiences should help the readers in chartering their own exclusive life trajectory of growth, success and contentment i.e. *Trupti.*

Raj Kanwar

Very eminent senior citizen of Dehra Dun, Veteran Journalist and Author

"I have read the script and found it relevant and interesting. The simple style is appealing and I am sure your young and upcoming readers would not only enjoy it but learn from your vast experience reflected in the work."

Dr. Usha Bande,

**(Formerly Professor and Head of Dept (English},
Himachal University, Shimla.)**

I am deeply grateful to her for sparing time for reviewing the "Know Thyself" draft in its early stage.

Krishan Aneja

ACKNOWLEDGEMENTS

I wonder where to begin for I am indebted to many individuals who helped me in pushing ahead with this endeavor.

Hon'ble DR. SANJEEV CHOPRA

The big question whom shall I request to review and write a foreword for 'Know Thyself' would regularly come up before me during the course of this journey but finding no satisfactory answer, it would get buried somewhere in mind. This dilemma persisted regularly but always no satisfying answer and the anxiety would take a pause and lie low. Many names always came up, but..........?

One day, sometimes in the year 2019, I met Shri Raj Kanwar, a prominent dignitary of the town, author and a reputed journalist, explained to him broadly the concept and central idea of 'Know Thyself' and requested him to suggest whom should I approach, besides he himself, for a review and writing of a Foreword for the book. Listening broadly to the theme of the book, he suggested only one name, that of Mr. Sanjeev Chopra. Google search made me wonder and anxious whether such a celebrated dignitary and highly busy literary giant would agree to spare time for it.

My dear friend, Sanjay, who has been helping me in many ways in this endeavor, had a chance to be with Dr. Chopra for 2, 3 days some years back on an official trip to Mumbai. During occasional discussions between us on this issue, my dear friend would suggest Chopra Saab's name and insist, "Let's try to meet him and make a request. He emphasized he still fondly remembers the soft, polite and a helpful temperament of Chopra Saab.

This relieved me of the mental pressure and one day, mustering courage and removing hesitancy from my mind, I called up Chopra Sir and made a request for a meeting for the purpose. Chopra Saab instantly affirmed and told the date, place and time for the meeting. For obvious reasons, I was hesitant and anxious while on our way but to be honest, when we met Chopra Saab, I was taken aback seeing him in plain simple attire, unlike for a very senior bureaucrat and a literary tycoon.

A multi-faceted and highly accomplished giant that he is, Chopra Saab reflects the persona of a sober, honest, and plain simple individual. He evokes instant respect while one inter-acts with him. Consequently, I felt relieved and mustered courage to be free and talk about the script and purpose of our meeting. He accepted my request and assured to review it and write the Foreword. Well, the Foreword is here now. It's in the public domain and I need not talk about it herein now.

The Foreword is a testimony, if one is required, of the super qualities of an honest and committed bureaucrat, dedicated literary giant, a straight forward historian, and a social reformist. I am partly aware that as Director of country's prestigious training academy for All India Service Officers, LBSNAA at Mussoorie, he was highly regarded as a committed reformist eager to motivate the up-coming officers with conviction for self-less service to the country and its citizen.

To be true to myself and frank, I find myself incapable of attempting to pen down Chopra Saab's varied achievements and contribution in literary world and umpteen fields of national importance.

He is a repository of accomplishments of high order, and a selflessly honest and a committed individual.

MR SANJAY MINOCHA

First of all, a very big sense of gratitude to him; but for his moral support and soothing words of appreciation of the broad concept, the thought/idea of 'Know Thyself' would have remained an idea in my mind only.

During the course of this long journey, Sanjay would often sit down with me and listen attentively to the topic(s) I had in mind or the script I had finished writing and suggest add-ons or changes to add value/depth to the idea/intent. His tacit appreciation of the contents of a chapter or the idea floating in my mind during his occasional presence has been a source of encouragement and moral strength for me. It kept me going ahead confidently. His suggestions/close involvement helped a lot in putting the chapters in proper sequence to maintain a meaningful and orderly flow of the content.

Earlier in 2014-15, when I was in the process of writing my autobiography, 'Karmath Jeevan', I being a novice in computer handling and writing, particularly the most important job of copy-pasting, I regularly took his help. He would visit regularly and make amends in the draft but for which book writing would have come to a halt. Later, the final format of the book presented by the Publishers was in bad shape. It was Sanjay who took upon himself the responsibility of giving it a final formatted structure and brought it up in an orderly lay-out. Sanjay's intervention had relieved me of the uncertainty of its publication. Indeed, his support and perseverance had been a source of strength for me.

He is a free-lance computer wizard, has to his credit accomplishing and launching successfully numerous books, journals and periodicals. His sober temperament and honest helpful attitude draw close to him regularly umpteen number of individuals and help seekers like me.

And last but not the least, it was he who came up with a suggestion to meet and request honorable Sanjeev Chopra Saab for writing a Foreword. I am happy we did it together and result is Chopra Saab's blessings in the Foreword.

All said and done, I am grateful, Sanjay, a big support to me, has always been by my side.

ABHISHEK GARG, a Young Technocrat, working in SAP, Bangalore

He is the son of my friend; Mr. Bipin Kumar. He is working in Bengaluru office of SAP but is in Dehra Dun now under the Work from Home Program. He not only helped me in handling technical glitches but also was frank in conveying his thoughts and meaningful views on the script.

He would come, go through the script during its early stages, discuss it and suggest changes/alterations in headings and presentation style to present it in a catchy and inter-active style; the purpose being to enthuse and draw the attention of the present day generation of youngsters like him and grown- ups alike.

He was candid in conveying that the concept and ideas contained in various chapters of 'Know Thyself' would be helpful to the readers for self development and growth.

In his frank discourse with me, he conveyed he felt enthused to have picked up meaningful messages/ concepts while going through the script.

KRISHNA ANEJA

The chapter on acknowledgements would be incomplete if I didn't acknowledge and bring up the role of meaningful occasional interactions I used to have with my better-half, Krishna.

Happily, she would spare time out of her busy household chorus and listen to the ideas floating in my mind and offer instantly her considered views thereon. A very sharp memory that she has been blessed with helped me to relook at some topics related to comments in the scriptures and/or views of our learned elders. Also, our interactions sometimes would bring up new approach and direction to the thoughts roaming in my mind at that time. Such interactions always encouraged me and added to my resolve to move ahead with confidence.

She is a blessed person in-as-much-as she is not only a loving and caring mother and a considerate life-partner but also a person of strong convictions. She would push ahead against odds and adversities when necessary. This aspect of her persona came to light in 1986, when I was posted outside Dehra Dun. Both our sons were school going then and she felt she had a lot of free time in the mornings till they came back around 2 O' clock. And she started a school on her own in one room in our house. She kept pushing ahead zealously and the school's strength reached at an incredible level of over 100 students. But for larger family's needs (both the sons were in USA), she had to visit them quite regularly. And with a heavy heart, the school had to be wound up in 2006.

Many times, she would wait patiently for evening tea/dinner while I used to be busy with this endeavor. Indeed, I am in debt to her for her open and meaningful support always.

SANDEEP ANEJA, our elder son

God's Grace, he is a well-established business tycoon of high standing and repute in his own right. Though an ever awfully busy individual in managing the affairs of his establishments, he would lend his ears to me and help sort out the issues/matters of my concerns for this endeavor. Free and frank discussions with him cleared the mist wherever and whenever I faced herein. His forthright comments and suggestions were useful in enhancing the depth and significance of many topics.

He has successfully completed the arduous task of editing of this book in spite of his extremely busy work schedules. Heartfelt thanks and gratitude to him for giving a fresh look to the script. Frankly, his super contribution in giving a final touch and hue to the book is beyond description.

Love him and wish him all the best in life. Surely the edited version has added to the depth of the script making it achieving its prime object: the object of facilitating the efforts of anxious and ambitious individuals to help them make their life journey poignant, promising and successfully satisfying.

MS. SHIVANI SINGH, OUR FIRST FLOOR NEIGHBOR

A nice, polite and smiling person, Shivani is an accomplished young 'Bachelor of Aerospace Engineering' from UPES, Dehra Dun. She has been a dependable source of help to me. During the initial stages of script writing I often felt an urge to seek the views of youngsters like her on the concept of the book and also the content. On my request, she would come down, go through the script and offer her frank views: a sort of confidence building measure for me.

She also helped me many times to overcome the bottleneck/problem I had been facing on my lap-top.

PROLOGUE

This book is neither a thesis nor a compilation of theories. It is a compilation of the rhythm of practical learning and knowledge acquired by me in the course of my happening life journey of eight decades including four decades of highly rewarding work-life. The intent is to share with the readers what is of real essence in shaping smoothly a purposeful life journey; both personal as well as professional.

The book lays out numerous practical steps, which when supplemented with professional competence/ knowledge and/or other higher academic learning can help the reader in preparing for a life journey that balances personal and professional ambitions: purpose being the advent of a highly rewarding, eventful and purposeful innings of life for self and society both.

Everyone welcome professional competence driven success at work. But, this alone cannot be the only component of a highly satisfying life journey. I believe: a purposeful life does comprise of a wider spectrum: not only self-satisfaction and recognition in the society but also evolution of one's inner-strength. This book brings up and discusses in depth the essence of 'knowing oneself well' to be able to realize one's full potential.

A healthy mind and inquisitive approach is a pre-requisite for securing a satisfying life innings. This book lays out the importance of self-analysis and critical attitude to lead and guide us in managing our life's affairs effectively. The book explains how self-motivation towards life as a whole arrived at through thoughtful and critical self analysis leads to approaching one's life in a comprehensive manner.

The book has been divided into four parts.

Part I discusses inputs of fundamental importance which help decipher and understand the nuances of a balanced and a rewarding life; a deep peep into important facets of life such as a positive and praiseworthy thought process and healthy value systems, which have the potential to help each one of us to acquire a distinct place in society.

Part II discusses the topics which are meant to help and serve as an add-on to one's professional knowledge and competence. The discussions are based on rich practical inputs/lessons picked by up me during the course of my journey. Part II also brings up and undertakes to discuss the subtle issues which impede the avowed objective of success and growth. It also highlights and discusses the important and certain commonly observed negative traits like misplaced ego, over-stretched ambitions and an attitude of harmful self-centered thought process.

Part III brings up an exercise of brain storming for self-appraisal and discusses defining stages in life and how to making life easy and stress free.

Part IV covers topics like the issues and anxieties associated with post-retirement life.

It is said, "Think beyond the possible." I believe that this is the cornerstone of a meaningful approach to life: focusing on life's value systems, its various meaningful attributes and fundamentals including post-retirement life and its impact on one's life.

The core discussions and idea of the book is to focus on a composite life: life consisting of personal life, work life and post-retirement phase of life.

Summing up; the book is intended to help invigorate the thought process and help the readers to charter their own exclusive trajectory of growth and success resulting in contentment (trupti).

MY IDENTITY

My life started virtually as a victim of circumstances and a destitute after I lost my father at the age of three and a half years. His departure left the family of seven in utter misery. Add to that the havoc played by the partition of the country in 1947, and you get a complete picture of absolute drudgery for the family. Growing up in harrowing circumstances after the family landed in India in September 1947, first in a refugee camp at Kurukshetra for about six months and later on in other different places, I struggled hard continuously to meet the challenges that my family faced in close succession. Beginning as a petty rent collector, a temporary, short-lived assignment on commission basis, I started exploring avenues for a regular government job after I passed my high school exam in 1952 and was successful in securing the job of a Goods Clerk in the Railways in 1956. The job of a Goods Clerk in railways then was thought to be a cherished career. I could have gone with the trend of the times and should have felt 'I have entered a career of choice and feel settled now.' Frankly speaking for a person from a lower middle-class family and a refugee, this job was quite attractive and could have defined my life. But it was not for me. The ray of ambition inside me and the advice of one of my elders encouraged me to pursue further studies to be eligible for a still higher grade job. From then on I decided to be a private student (non-college going) while working as a clerk.

Thus began a lifetime of pursuing greater ambitions in my life despite the odds. I passed the undergraduate program (BA) of Punjab University as a private candidate and this led me to switch from one job to another until I felt I had made a real beginning. That occurred when I joined Bokaro Steel Ltd, as an Executive in 1972. It was an opportunity of great significance as from then on, multiple avenues of growth opened for me.

Not giving up too early in the face of adversity was a key to reaching my target.

In hindsight, this growth happened due to two factors: my restless ambitious personality which kept on pushing me ahead and a '*Guru Mantra*' that my mother had given to me: "People don't care for your skin; they like and want performance/results. (*Kisi ko bhi tumhara chaam nahin, kaam pyara hota hai.*). I followed this edict religiously throughout my work-life and was successful in delivering more than what was expected. The result was there for everyone to see; from a petty rent collector in 1954 I rose to the position of General Manager (Finance) in the prestigious national oil company, the Oil & Natural Gas Corporation Ltd.(ONGC) in 1991, from where I superannuated honorably in the year 1994 at the age of 58.

Moral: Be aware of your circumstances, determine clearly what you expect from life, pursue education rigorously and acquire competence and skills, demonstrate through your performance that you are dependable, and do not relax until you achieve the target you have set for yourself.

Be determined and continue to excel, surprising even yourself.

MY LEARNING STEPS

Let me briefly sum up and share with you the prime sources of inspiration and fateful learning that guided me.

The most important was my habit of acting on intuitions and affirmative inner calls which appeared to be relevant to the occasion and which, as per my gut feeling appeared to me to be opportunities of consequence.

One might wonder how my ambitious personality took shape. I believe; my mother's unique responsible parenting under the harshest circumstances inspired me. And stories from my father's life, as told to me by my mother, taught me to never compromise on my principles. In addition to these, the noble acts of several elders in the family during my formative years molded my thoughts and actions in a positive direction. Later on in life, the deeds and inspirational acts of some role-models and mentors went a long way in making me who I am today.

I believe being super observant, curious and open minded helped me benefit from the lessons thrown at me.

Finally, the lessons learnt in the company of my buddies in Shimla during my early twenties during passionate discussions on various subjects and thought provoking ideas on life added a strong head start to my eventful life. Picking a nurturing, intellectually stimulating peer group with shared ethos and values played a significant role in shaping me as a young man. Some of those friendships are dear to me even today.

To sum up, the serendipitous incidents, spontaneous intuitions, the inspired ambition, fueled by hard work along with my passionate will to beat my own and my superiors' expectations of performance resulted in continuous growth in my career. My consistent approach was to perform well so as to make my seniors reliant on me for consistently high-quality work. "Perform well and leave the burden of growth on seniors' shoulders. I was not wrong and believe me with this simplistic thinking, I was able to achieve growth even in the government sector, which is well known for nepotism.

I enjoyed being recognized as a workaholic, a dependable and committed performer. I did feel proud to be singled out for appreciation, when due.

It is said, "Lady Luck smiles and knocks on each individual's door randomly. It is for the individuals to recognize the opportunity knocking at the door. Those who understand the call and seize it, never look back."

INTRODUCTION

Human Beings: the Star Creation

Ancient Hindu mythology says that being born as a human being is God's benign 'Krupa' for those who deserve it. Although humans' self-destructive tendencies are top of the news headlines nowadays, yet our species has a distinct hue and identity. We are blessed with brain that has a uniquely strong ability to conceive, mull and introspect.

The Oxford dictionary defines the brain as the mind or intellect and intelligence. Of all the species on this planet, the human beings have been uniquely blessed with advanced capabilities to judge and evaluate a situation in a calibrated manner. What happens when a person remains substantively ignorant of the creative potential of the brain? Lala Hardayal, an Indian revolutionary and a freedom fighter said, "If you do not use your brain to the utmost of your power, you are more akin to the beast than to Homo sapiens."

I believe: this gift is not without responsibility either. Being the exclusive repository of instinct to introspect, rationally think and visualize, human beings are expected to use it with discretion and logic: use it not only for personal good but also for the wellbeing of others including other creatures and nature at large: flora, fauna, jungles, mountains, glaciers and our vast water bodies. However most of us have abdicated this responsibility towards the larger good. And most of us tend to overlook the consequences. The disturbing trend is that a majority of us remain focused on personal good only. Some of us actively participate in the flagrant misuse of the natural resources resulting in disastrous consequences for all. While there is a shared sense of clarity on what is to be achieved, there is a collective loss of accountability and an increase in either transferring blame or playing the victim.

While we possess a sense of collective ownership, I believe it is not a reflection of sum-total of our individual self-awareness. Being self-aware helps us to be more rational, more humble, more focused and more humane. Every individual has a clear choice to make and often these choices, made en-masse, create a collective societal conscience: shifting this conscience towards a goal that helps us be better individuals while making our planet more livable for all species.

I believe; self-awareness, being rational and humane is the primary response expected of the Star Creation by HIM.

It is rightly said; "Just stand by and suffer humility or stand up and get going confidentially,"

Humans' Unique Strength; Positive Thought Process

Thought is one of the greatest powers that human beings possess. There is nothing good or bad but thinking makes it so.

Swami Vivekananda once said, "Thoughts live, they travel far." Simply put, thoughts help and possess the power of bringing change within oneself and those around us.

While thinking clearly is hard enough, what is harder is auditing one's own thinking. Getting to the point of auditing one's thought process requires the ability to be a "fly on the wall", looking into the thoughts, both conscious and less-conscious, objectively. While, in my youth, I was too impatient to sit down and examine my thinking deeply, as I grew older, I found meditation to be a powerful ally in my self-discovery journey. Meditation is the unique important off-shoot of the thought process. It is one's inner journey in an endeavor to focus on the important while letting go of the unimportant, the distraction. It is a process of focused cleansing of thoughts to give the body, mind, and the soul enough rest so as to allow new thoughts to form more actively, irrelevant ones to be abandoned and, overall, better clarity to prevail. It's an opportunity for deep self-realization. Meditation, when accomplished successfully; results in tranquility and peace of mind; the attributes which are essential for life.

Thoughts represent everyone's unique characteristics. Believing in self and seeking help from others to better understand which thought is likely to lead to fulfillment is the key for self-realization. Self-realization helps build up self-confidence, overcome inhibitions and lay a sound foundation built on awareness as opposed to assumptions. Such an exercise also provides the stimulus to efforts in overcoming obstacles.

Basically, the drill of knowing the self without any illusions or under any other similar influences provides a framework of values and objectives to our decision making faculties.

Quite often, we worry too much about others' feelings about us. This clouds our faculties of thought and action. How others see us doesn't matter as more often than not they are more focused on themselves and we, likely, matter very little to them. How we see ourselves means everything. Understanding oneself means knowing ourselves in the present, our value systems and approach to life. This is the foundation to being objectively able to analyze what motivates us, drives us and concerns us and only then does it make sense to plan ahead.

Summing up, the exercise of knowing self enables us to be balanced and pragmatic in conducting our daily affairs. It enables us to know the truth and make necessary changes, and also helps us in taking meaningful steps to be able to utilize our potential effectively. Quite often in a mad rush of chasing success, a vast majority of people, including highly qualified professionals and managers tend to believe that they know themselves well and do not need to self-examine or change anything. This attitude has serious implications. For, such an assumption could be a shallow act of self-indulgence.

Ignorance of one's true values is nothing but deceiving one-self. Overlooking the obvious has its own perils: Help your-self in being objective and realistic.

PART I

CHAPTER 1

LIFE'S INTRINSIC VALUES AND HAPPENINGS

Introspection: a Prime Help in Self-realization

The Oxford dictionary says introspection is "examination of one's own thoughts and feelings"

Our scriptures suggest that introspection is not just confined to this simple process. Scriptures tell us that introspection means dwelling deeply within self and concentrating on super values in an endeavor to firm up our resolve to give a new meaning to our will-power and to move ahead in life on principles. When taken up as a regular routine in life, introspection helps discover clean options and how to put them to use in day to day life. Following this, no wonder, then life chugs merrily along the path of serene satisfaction. Of course, being satisfied doesn't mean being inactive or adopting an attitude of laissez-faire. Keep pushing ahead, as before, with self-confidence guided by inner-calls and nuances of integrity and fairness. Get charged with enthusiasm and learn how to make calibrated moves forward on the path to glory and bigger success. Work hard to be able to evolve self in sync with this effort. This is the true meaning of a successful innings in this universe.

A pure and clean mind is said to be the favorite habitat for constructive ideas to germinate. This condition in a human being's life is the first step on the path towards the birth of a sublime and higher thinking process which, as we all know, has the potential to make our journey fulfilling and sweet. Don't worry; true success keeps following then, on its own.

Core Belief and its Role in Life

Core belief is bunch of personal values of an individual. It is a bunch of solemn traits which lie ensconced in one's inner-self. They get built up and strengthened further in the course of each individual's life. Core belief can also be said to be one's rhythm of life: always soothing and ready to guide and lead in man's quest for fulfillment/satisfaction.

Can one add and enrich these values? Yes, first and foremost by being positive and satisfied with one's lot, by Swadhyay, (committed self-learning) of scriptures/holy books, by being inquisitive about learning it from family elders and other learned thinkers/scholars by reading specific books, journals and magazines, by listening to holy men/women in the group counseling sessions, and by discussions with like-minded persons. The Seeker (yourself) has to take a view about the choice(s) and where to begin from. And this will depend upon one's inclination of mind and the company he/she keeps.

Avenues for picking up values are not difficult to find but only an inquisitive mind can have access to them. One need not pursue many options at a time. Pick up the one which you think is feasible for you. After all, in today's highly competitive world when even survival is at stake, one cannot be expected to neglect one's profession/job etc.

The Value System

It means a bunch of basic values and principles that lead and guide us. It is believed that while one inherits some values by birth, some others are acquired initially under the influence of core members of the family especially the mother. A mother is said to be the first Guru of a child. Her influence inspires the child the most and lays the foundation for child's value-system. The other elders in the family being closely associated also inspire the child with their conduct and teachings. In a way, the family as a whole serves as a role model for the child. In addition, the teachers, fellow students, friends, media, the environment and dominant happenings in society also play an important role in a person's life. The foundation thus laid forms a core strength for the child who later, as an adolescent and grown up individual makes use of it and adds to it with his/her own ability and experiences.

It is universally acknowledged that the values one is equipped with determine one's conduct in life. Values form life's foundation. They shape our life. Depending upon their inherent nature, they bring glory and make the journey meaningful and smooth or bring disrepute making life miserable.

The spectrum of values is vast in a human being's life. Values are not static by nature. They can be enriched with conscious efforts and keen observational attitude. It is the individual himself/herself who being the '*Karta*' can realize the potential of his/her value system and enrich them with perseverance.

Sanskars (संस्कार)

Sanskars are referred to as the healthy and balanced values which help and guide the individuals in conducting the affairs of life with equanimity. It is the mainstay, an axis on which the wheel of life's journey runs. Humans only have been blessed with capability to acquire and develop this virtuous trait. It's an exclusive bliss for us. Its resting place is our inner-self.

Sanskars, the healthy values set the agenda and purpose of life/birth for an individual. Shorn of healthy values, human beings lose their identity as such and then there remains no perceptible difference between human beings and other creatures. Healthy values are the essence of life, a super compendium of rich thoughts. A life without them is shallow, rather non-descript. Healthy values guide the individual to carry out diligently and meaningfully the affairs of life and beyond. It is a precious treasure which needs to be protected from wild attacks of negative sentiments.

For discerning and inquisitive minds and eyes, the process of learning and accumulating the rich values never ends. It is a continuous life-long process. Simply put, up-dating and up-grading of human values is as important, rather a critical necessity, as is updating/upgrading the technological programs, equipment and physical facilities for innovation and improvement.

Healthy values, as the name suggests, is a treasure trove of inspiring traits. It is an asset of immense value for any individual. As they say about education, a healthy value system once developed and perfected can neither be stolen nor does it diminish over a period of time.

This treasure lies ensconced deep in the inner-self, gets strengthened with the passage of time and gets polished continuously on its own. With time, it grows exponentially and becomes more sophisticated with the help of new values picked up in the course of our journey of life.

Healthy values deeply influence our basic approach to life and serve as a sound foundation for various faculties to get strengthened. They have the potential to strengthen one's core beliefs, the gene and the vision. They bring in their wake a willing attitude, compassion and sensitivity to understand others' pains and difficulties rather easily.

The opposite of what is stated above are the negative and reprehensible values which lead to an offending conduct resulting in difficulties and problems in life. The dynamics of entire process are fairly complex. Be on the guard and vigilant, lest the treasure trove of healthy values gets polluted under the influence of negative but seemingly attractive values.

Sanskar vs Ahankar (Arrogance)

While Sanskars help us being rational, arrogance (ahankar) vitiates one's thought process. An old couplet, given below, explains that while ahankar (ego) brings up an urge for letting others down, sanskars render one humble and pave the way for self-satisfaction.

> "Ahankar aur sanskar mein furk hai
>
> Ahankar doosre ko jhuka kar khush hota hai
>
> Sanskar swyem ko jhuka kar khush hota hai"

Annonymous

An Inner Call Vs an Intuition

What is an inner call? I believe; it is a call from one's conscience hence an honest fateful calling. An inner call is a sublime guide. Its value is supreme and sacrosanct. It surfaces only when one is at peace with self and is in a care free serene state of mind. When it surfaces, one has to churn and mull to find the message behind it. it is said, 'an inner call, if it happens, when one is seeking solace and shelter in isolation in an endeavor to connect with self, is the most opportune help for achieving the goal.'

In mundane activities of life, the inner call helps in either solving a given problem or for making a fresh move of substance or feeling relieved of a dilemma. An inner call leads and helps in being master of the prevailing confusing circumstances, if any.

As against this, an intuition is described as 'the power of knowing or understanding something immediately without reasoning or being taught.' Since an intuition is said to be without reasoning it may or may not prove to be helpful, may or may not be opportune and relevant in a given situation. Against this, an inner call is a much deeper phenomenon coming as it does from one's inner-self which is said to be a repository of rich values not prone to external influences. The vibrations and signals received then surely help crystallize the message behind the inner call and help in firming up the future course of action. An inner call is benign and is said to be a message of supreme value.

Musings (चिंतन)

Passion

"Knowledge of mankind is knowledge of their passion."

Benjamin Disraeli

Passion means a sense of madness, craze or 'Junoon' (in Urdu) forcing the individual to work with determination and zeal for accomplishing the task in hand or achieving the target in mind.

It's a forceful propeller pushing ambitious individuals to accelerate efforts; efforts in the right direction. In Hindi, it is also called 'unmad' or 'sanak' which literally mean a stage of madness and craziness not willing to look back or give up without achieving the goal. Yes, without a crazy mind or a sense of madness, passion remains a wishful idea only.

Harness the passion, cultivate determination and muster essential inputs and you will find the goal is not far off. Keep pushing for now you are sure to achieve what you had thought of. The goal is not a dream now. It's a reality out there to surprise you.

Performance always

Comes from passion and not from pressure,

Always be passionate.

Love what you do, do what you love.

Success is yours.

Burning desire to excel

The Oxford dictionary says, "To excel oneself means to do better than one has ever done before."

By itself, the burning desire is limitless. It eliminates inhibitions in mind, if any. It knows no boundaries. Combined with passion, it overpowers one's mind and burns away reservations/doubts, if any. The deadly combination of passion and desire to excel opens up the realms of great success and excellent achievements. What is normally seen as impossible, burning desire makes it possible and achievable. It's an additive which fuels one's determination and the will to overcome the inhibitions and obstacles. Burning desire is a forceful ingredient for churning of thoughts. It pushes the passion into the realms of excellence.

A compelling and burning desire to excel brings up on its own the requisite extra energy for meeting the challenge one is face to face with. It helps create an urge to push ahead: push beyond the normal, beat the competition and create an exclusive niche for the idea/ product in mind.

Just desiring and wishing only are like, "if wishes were horses, beggars would ride."

Inferiority complex vs. Superiority complex

Literally, complex means something abnormal and harmful. Whereas a sense of inferiority leads to lack of self-confidence leading to a state of helplessness in mind, the sense of superiority leads to a sense of over-confidence in self. Obviously, both are of negative nature. The sense of inferiority would destroy initiative and lead to a sense of fear of failure and disrepute. And the sense of superiority would most likely lead to a sense of lull and lack of initiative for venturing into difficult terrain. Laissez-faire clouds the vision leading to a sense of inaction and surrender.

Of the two, can one be accepted as a valid option? No, I believe, both are negative. One needs to be self-confident and enthusiastic about one's potential to overcome the complex, if any. Successful innings in life are possible only if one believes in self and is capable of warding off any feeling of inferiority or superiority. It's far easier to achieve progress and excel if one is free of any such thought. Free and open mind only can visualize a valid and optimum option when face to face with a dilemma. Therefore, do not entertain any sense of superiority or inferiority. Nobody is inferior or superior as such. It's the thinking that makes it so.

Some people accept and believe superiority complex as relevant for growth because the phrase 'superior' denotes a praiseworthy connotation. Well, is it a balanced assessment? No, because in the end, it would turn out to be false and misleading.

A complex, whether of a superiority or of inferiority shade, is derogatory. Complex denotes a complicated set of mind. A complex free mind only can visualize openness of one's thought process enabling the individual to pick up an optimum and an aggressive line of action, where necessary.

Concluding, it is fair to suggest that in the interest of a balanced and forward looking life, one should shake off complexes, if any, empower the thought process to wade through obstacles, if any, and keep pushing ahead till the goal is achieved.

Ego be damned

Ego has been defined as the self-esteem, conceit. Nothing wrong about it for self-esteem and conceit are neutral and balanced in themselves. It is only when these attributes are flaunted to others to convey own self-assumed superiority, they become reprehensible. Generally, in common parlance, ego is referred to as a negative trait and often it is said that ego is a damaging attribute of life. Therefore, one has to be cautious in dealings. Be circumspect in dealings and take care to be balanced. After all, self-esteem and conceit by themselves do not signify any negative qualities. It is the careless attitude that leads to conflict in the mind of others.

"Where there is no ego, there is no suffering."

Ramayana

"Anger is one of the signs of egotism."

Swami Rama Krishnananda

"When you drop the ego, you drop a whole world that you have created around you. For the first time you are able to see things as they are-not as you would like them to be,"

Osho

"Mita dey apni hsti ko, agar kutch martba chahiye, ki dana khak mein mil kar gule gulzar hota hai."

The above quoted Urdu couplet means "shun your egos if you desire to achieve success and an enviable position in life; for a seedling can grow as a lovely beautiful flower only from dust/mud.

"Shun self-aggrandizement; know thyself well, be careful while dealing with others, build up a persona capable of taking a balanced view of life and thus be able to secure an honorable standing/position in society. Do not super-impose yourself anytime anywhere.

The Oxford dictionary defines ego as, "the self, self-esteem, conceit," and egotism as, "the practice of talking too much about one-self, conceit." One can think, what's wrong with self-indulging? After all, if I do not care about myself and my views, who else will? Yes, there is nothing wrong in an individual believing in self and being confident of knowing one-self fully well. The real problem is being conceited and aggressive.

"Khudi ko kar buland itna, ki har taqdeer se pehle,
Khuda bande se khud poochey bata teri raza kya hai"

Allama Iqbal

I have dared to pick up this heart-rending couplet from my memory lane but wonder if I am able to do justice to it and touch the depth of it. It has been close to my heart and rotating in my mind since long.

With due respects to Allama, I venture to present my understanding of it. To me it conveys, "Build up your self-esteem so high that when the Lord decides to bestow HIS Blessings on you, HE asks you before-hand, "What is your will and choice?" Well, it can be said, "It's not normal for normal human beings." Yes, it is an extremely difficult proposition but all the same it is within the realms of possibility. A genuine high level of equitable vision, super deep balanced thoughts and benign conduct do make it possible.

A couplet in Hindi proclaims, "Jin khojeya tin paya gehre pani baith."

My understanding, though not sufficient, of it would be; "Super deep thoughts and solemn vision only can enable us to pursue and achieve lofty goals."

One would wonder if it can be within one's reach. True, it is acutely difficult but possible only if one shuns self-ego, his/her mind is free of conceit and his/her dealings and acts are pliable. Do to others what you would do to yourself.

"Neki kar darya main dal"

Literally, it conveys:" Do a selfless act of welfare, public good and extend a helping hand to others but selflessly." Be helpful to the needy and forget about it. Do not boast about it. Entertain in mind no expectation of a reciprocal hand for service of the downtrodden and needy is the service of God. Selfless help to the needy is the ultimate satisfaction in life. Such an act enriches one's value system and is blessed by HIM.

"Pehle tolo, phir bolo"

Be careful and make sure, what you are going to speak is harmless and free of malice for anyone. My primary class teacher had explained it thus, 'what you speak should be without any glitches and ill-will. Plain talk without any hidden meaning behind it is always acceptable by all.

While speaking with elders and distinguished members of the society begin with regards and continue in respectful manners till last.'

The class teacher used to add, 'As a general precaution, don't use offending or high sounding proverbs/idioms etc. in your talk. Beware, frank conversation elicits frank response and helps solve the issues, if any, amicably.'

"Parsai, Khudai se Doosre Darje par Hai"

"Cleanliness is next to Godliness"

Our primary class teacher used to repeat it quite often, "Clean and pure housing (our body) is the abode of clean thoughts/behavior. Be an early riser. Laziness leads to dullness and lack of positive energy/ enthusiasm.

His pet and favorite lines in Urdu were," Subah hua jab noor ka tadka, so kar utha achha ladka." Which meant the good boy wakes up early morning when the sun spreads its glow in the universe. The good boy takes his bath etc. and gets ready to welcome the new day." Next step, "Say your prayers, bow to Lord ALMIGHTY and convey your respects to HIM. Prayers conveyed humbly with an open mind from the core of heart do reach HIM and augur well for the day."

Knowledge

"The more you know yourself, the more clarity there is. Self-knowledge has no end- you don't come to an achievement, you don't come to a conclusion. It is an endless river."

Jiddu Krishnamurthy

"Knowledge is like a deep well fed by perennial springs, and your mind is the little bucket that you drop into it: you will get as much as you can assimilate."

Lala Hardayal

The sum total of knowledge is to 'Know Thyself' fully well. Life's journey of each individual is guided by what he/she believes to be true, desirable and worthy of emulation. It's essential, therefore, to beware of one's bent of mind, beliefs and aspirations. Determine, what you think to be right is really right. Do not rush to conclusion without application of due process of validity check. Our thoughts and acts are influenced and guided by the company one keeps. They say a person is known by the company he/she keeps. Human beings are said to be like apes; follow what others are doing. This tendency of blindly following others needs to be kept under check for obvious reasons. Be your normal self always; avoid rash acts and hiccups for your life journey to be smooth and satisfying.

Handling Problems of Life

Irrespective of the nature and size of the problem one needs to be focused and passionate to be able to take a balanced and calibrated view. An attitude of self-reprimand and control, when necessary, is also helpful in solving a problem. Rather, it is necessary. A focused mind provides strength to one's character; a vital input for being able to handle problems with ease. Also, a strong and focused mind generates a huge amount of self-confidence. When faced with a problem, one tends to excuse oneself under the garb of some alibi and start pointing an accusing finger at others. Such a thought comes to mind as a first response quite easily. Indeed, it is a very tempting option to relieve oneself of the burden of self-appraisal. Why, because it tends to lighten the burden of guilt and props up a justification for one's act of not accepting the real position. Once one falls into this trap, arrogant behavior becomes a justifiable norm in conduct and gradually settles down in psych as a valid option. But remember; an arrogant person makes more foes than friends, gets isolated and loses respect in society. Further consequences are obvious; always being tense and under mental fatigue.

Adversities

Adversity introduces a man to him/herself. Adversity means unfavorable circumstances which are prone to getting afflicted with misfortune or are likely to result in harm. But it is nothing unusual if one faces adverse and difficult situations which threaten to destabilize and push us away from our comfort zone. When face to face with such a situation, do not lose heart. Strike back with full determination and preparedness. Face them with conviction if you mean to be successful. There is no escape. It is no use blaming others, stars, circumstances or society at large. This attitude doesn't help. In fact, it is meaningless to seek shelter behind such illusions. History tells us that all great leaders and icons faced adversities in one form or the other but met them with determination and came out successful.

How can one think of ameliorating one's lot without overcoming the obstacles? True, the bigger the adversity, the bigger would have to be the effort to over-come it. Notwithstanding the adverse circumstances, one can and should aspire for growth. Believe in self: make optimum use of own potential with single-minded determination and work ceaselessly hard to push ahead. Do not look back. Success beckons those who believe in self.

Let's follow the dictum of **"Karma"** as revealed by **Lord Krishna** in the "**Gita**"

"He who does the task,

Dictated by duty,

Caring nothing,

For the fruit of action,

He is a Yogi".

Is it surprising then that many victims of circumstances like the refugees during the partition of India in 1947 made a new beginning rather soon in an extremely adverse environment? They had no capital but believed in the veracity of '*Karma*'. The territory they landed in was different, faced hostile response from vast majority of local people, and suffered the ignominy of discrimination. Even proper and meaningful interaction was a problem due to language barrier. Ignoring all these adversities, they worked tirelessly and determinedly hard to make a new beginning but never stretched their hands before others for alms. Of course, as a matter of right, they did fight with authorities for support and help and succeeded in creating a place of respect for themselves in the new territory. This is just one example but nonetheless full of deeper meanings and lessons for vast population.

Our family was no exception. Our elders faced the adverse circumstances with determination ignoring all the obstacles even if it meant suffering the pangs of hunger and sustaining ourselves with bare necessities of life with no compromise on principles of self respect. We, the children, were strictly prohibited from giving vent to any signs of deprivation.

The conclusion: Adversities teach us big lessons. They sharpen our skills of being courageous, self-confident and brave. They build ability to stand tall in calamities even unleashed by nature. Easy and smooth life fails to groom. So, ignore all the obstacles, worry not about some adverse comments of others, persist in your efforts and create an opening for yourself in your own unique way.

Good humor, cool temperament are assets of great significance. Some setbacks need not deter or weaken resolve.

CHAPTER 2

BENIGN FUNDAMENTALS OF LIFE

TRUTH

"What is truth? A difficult question; but I have solved it by saying that what the 'voice within' tells you."

"The seeker after truth should be humbler than the dust."

Mahatma Gandhi

We all are very well aware of the courage, determination and inner strength with which Mahatma Gandhi successfully led the Nation and secured for India a place of respect for it in the comity of Nations.

The Oxford dictionary defines truth as "the quality of being true." And true is defined as "in accordance with fact and in accordance with correct principles of an accepted standard: "genuine and not false.""

Truth is the keel on which an inspiring and luminous edifice of life rests. When adopted in life, these principles defined as true and rightly so make human beings free of

59

fear, inhibitions and similar other base feelings/notions. It is said, "Truth ultimately prevails though there may be some hiccups and unsavory deplorable situations sometime."' This dictum is a universal truth common to all cultures and societies. The leading figures all over the globe have been following it in their lives. Countless names prop up while reminiscing on this issue.

Why some people do not seek shelter beneath truth's benign umbrella? They probably fear being losers while treading on this path. Unknown fear, greed and ego take the center-stage and lets human beings deprive themselves of the place of honor and individuality in society. Such persons ignore the lofty principles of being up right, fair and honest: honest to themselves in the first place and also to the others as a whole.

Truth and truthful conduct provide courage and strength. They make us free of the fear of the Unknown and possible unsavory reactions. While on the path of truth, anxieties about future fade away. The focus then is on real picture and peace of mind takes charge. On the contrary, the prevalent mood in society at large is in favor of smartness in dealings and personal conduct. All over, a hectic race devoid of truth and honest principles seems to be the norm. On the other hand, those who follow the path of truthfulness are looked down upon with suspicion and are subjected to delirious responses. Forgive me, my intention is neither to sermonize nor is it an attempt to establish my credentials as a proponent of any creed. I am a common man who tried hard to remain focused on an honest and positive disposition always. My mother set an example before me and I followed her. I am happy I did it.

Let me confess, "Even if I make an attempt to tell a lie, I miserably fall short of ideas as to how to coin and deliver the falsehood." I tell myself, 'Leave it. It is beyond you and I feel relieved.'

Prayer: Mankind's Mainstay

The Oxford dictionary defines prayer as a 'solemn request or thanksgiving to God or object of worship'. To me, 'solemn request' means praying to God for seeking a boon or blessings for success and/or peace of mind. Thanksgiving denotes gratitude after a solemn request has been granted by Him. Let's remember the solemn truth; He is the Creator, He is the Creator/Preserver and He is the Destroyer of this universe. Nothing is beyond Him. He is Omnipresent and Omnipotent. *He is the "Aadi" and He is the "Ant".*

Not getting into a debate, I would suggest; pray to Him if you have faith in Him & His propensity of bestowing good on all, humanity's welfare, granting wishes and listening to prayers. Do it willfully, if and when do with genuine humbleness, 'Shradhha' and regularity. Do not skip it. How you do it is your choice but be careful about the manner in which you perform it. Serene, peaceful environment and clean and an exclusive place in the house are a pre-requisite so that you can concentrate well and try to connect with Him.

Many youngsters believe, prayers better be postponed to old age. No, there is no age bar for attempting to connect with HIM. Also, many youngsters believe and expect prayers to be answered instantly. How mistaken this notion is. Every deed/action has its unique gestation period. Prayers are such a lofty and noble act of which an affirmative response should not be anticipated. Prayers oozing out of bottom of soul do help. In fact, one will not know when the prayer is accepted. Have faith. It is a soothing surprise always. One thing is for sure; prayers leave a trail of happiness and peace of mind. Believe in HIM and try to connect with HIM any time anywhere.

You don't need to spend lot of time in prayers. You are very busy and not able to spare time for it? No problem. Salute Him and solemnly pray while going to or coming back from work and make up on week-ends. If this also is not possible sometimes, express your gratitude and convey thanks to Him first thing after you get up in the morning and just before going to sleep. Do it with all the humbleness and gratitude in your heart.

Prayers even if done for a few minutes with genuine attitude do reach Him. Every religion acknowledges that He is Omnipresent.

My mother used to say, "He listens to every prayer and grants the wish if there is no malaise in it." She would go a step further and tell, "Do not seek boons for your-self alone. Request Him for His Blessings for all. Remember, you are part of all."

Prayers grant us peace and strength of mind, solemn energy and zeal to overcome adversities with equanimity. A sense of satisfaction, fulfillment and gratefulness become a part of our psych which plays an important role in moving ahead in life, gracefully and with poise.

What if you proclaim you are an atheist? Be happy as you are. May be, some day you realize He is the Benefactor for all mankind, acknowledge His graceful existence and omnipotence. Then on, make prayers your daily routine.

Mother: An Angel for the Child

In mythology, the mother is placed on a high pedestal and rightly so.

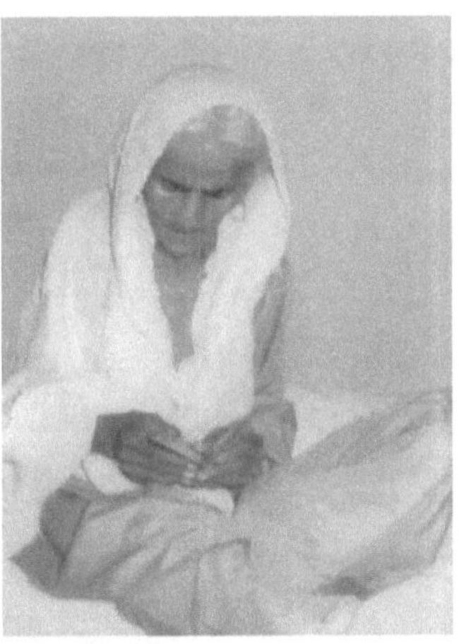

Being the 'Janani', she is deeply in love with her progeny. Taking good care of her loved ones is her second nature. She is the provider, 'Annapurna' not only for her children but the entire family. She is the protector and willingly ignores herself and suffers, if required, for the welfare of her children. Sacrifice in the interest and well-being of her children is no sacrifice for her. The perennial treasure of love in heart that she is blessed with by the Lord transmutes into solemn duty towards her children.

The example of my mother's life is the source of such thinking. After the day's difficult chores, she used to be by our side in the evening to make us comfortable in our beds. She would sing a lullaby or a devotional song or narrate an episode from a holy 'granth' along with massaging our foreheads to make sure that we were comfortable and slept peacefully. It touches my heart deeply even today when I recall her self-effacing love for us.

A mother is always anxious about her children's well-being. The children, even when they grow up and get married or remain busy in their own affairs, continue to be her prime focus. Regular and timely phone calls from her children living far off is all that she expects to receive. She would hesitate to convey the information of her illness lest it distracts the child, believing she will be alright soon.

A mother has greater influence on her children and is, therefore, better placed to influence and guide them.

A mother is the prime influence on the child and this puts a big responsibility on her shoulders, the responsibility to ensure that her influence is healthy, positive and deep rooted and serves as a beneficial and meaningful prop in her child's interest. Beware; a mother has no self-interest vis-à-vis her progeny. Watching her children grow up as young adolescents and adults is the most fulfilling desire for her. Believe me; we the males are pygmies in comparison to her in so far as our children are concerned.

CHAPTER 3

LIFE - AN ETERNAL SAGA

Life Is

A Rainbow

The colors of rainbow refer to and represent different moods and feelings. Broadly, these colors are identified with a feeling of love, passion, energy, happiness, hope, deceit, abundance, honesty, truth, intuition, inner mind and consciousness.

Like rainbow, our life too is an arch/bunch 0f colors: like colors of love, happiness, hope, truth, feelings of plenty, hilarious inner feeling, sense of satisfaction (trupti), feeling of achievement and fulfillment of an ambition etc. brought up on various occasions by the circumstances, happenings and events. On each such occasion, our psych gets affected and creates a world of different moods and thoughts in our mind. The varying streams of thoughts take charge of the situation unfolding at a given occasion. Depending upon the emerging scenario, our mind happens to bring up unconsciously different moods and shades before us. Each such situation gets reflected in our response to it with varying moods similar to colors of a rainbow.

A Full Life

"We live in deeds, not years: in thoughts, not breaths: in feelings, not in figures on a dial. We should count time by heart throbs. He most lives who thinks most, feels the noblest, and acts the best.

Aristotle

The meaning of life as summed up above by the great philosopher and thinker is compelling enough for deeper thoughts and gently invigorates one's inner-self. It conveys that a life which is full of noble thoughts, feelings and actions only is a meaningful life. Only such a life can be said to fully justify its existence.

Life: A Bunch of Creative Faculties

The Creator of the Universe has endowed human beings with faculties of conceiving, dispassionately mulling and analyzing objectively varying situations unfolding from time to time. These faculties lead us and help determine our basic approach to life by bringing to our attention the assorted bunch of thoughts, moods and influences. In turn, such thoughts etc. help us in correctly shaping the course of our journey. An individual, who manages his/her life under their positive influence and sublime guidance, his/her life is blessed with happiness, satisfaction and peace of mind. However, who get tempted to ignore these callings and take recourse to a negative approach like jealousy, greed and revenge etc. under the influence of some other seemingly attractive alternatives are ultimately the losers: losers of peace of mind and denial of a peaceful living.

Life: A Challenge and Opportunity Both

The Oxford dictionary describes challenge 'a call to demonstrate one's ability or strength' amongst others, which means one is expected to respond effectively when confronted with such a call. I believe, no challenge is too big for a determined mind. Be self confident and bold. A challenge is a challenge only till you are not willing to face it. Find out its contours, its depth and its implications for you. Having done so, determine the course of action necessary to beat it and then build up your response with conscious efforts to convert it into an opportunity. Remember, life is not only challenges. Life is also full of opportunities for creative minds. It is said, 'Lady Luck smiles with a knock on each door randomly.' Beware:"It is a knock of an opportunity: an opportunity of significant value." Those who understand the knock and grasp the opportunity by making an appropriate move with confidence are rewarded with success by readily launching their efforts in the right direction. Do not be impatient. Let your efforts take reasonable time to fructify.

There is a saying in Hindi, '*Sakal Padarath Hain Jag Maheen, Bhagye Heen Nar Pawat Naheen.*' which means, this universe is full of opportunities but unlucky are those who are not able to identify them, seize them and exploit them in their favor.'

Life: A Nectar

The Oxford Dictionary defines Nectar as "the drink of Gods", "a sweet fluid produced by plants and collected by bees for making honey." Who wouldn't want to savor nectar but is it freely available?' No, one cannot just wish and aspire to drink it. First, toil like bees to identify the opportunity and then struggle to collect it.

Our life can be sweet like nectar only if we struggle hard first to identify the promising opportunity and then follow it by appropriate toil to grab it.

Life: Grit, Guts and Gumption

Grit is courage and endurance, guts represent fundamental, basic approach and gumption is common sense and initiative. Combined together, these explosive, meaningful attributes are the core upon which one can build a high mansion of choice. Therefore, the aspirants of phenomenal rise, high growth and rewarding success in life have to first wriggle out of complacence and internalize these qualities. Having done it, firm up your fundamental basic approach laced with conviction, prudence and coupled with patience and endurance.

Beware: the deadly combination of these superlative qualities gives new meaning and new direction to life. Go ahead, nothing can stop you now. Those who have internalized these attributes with conviction can hope to secure what others may call it a dream. No hurdle is acceptable to such individuals/groups in their spirited march on the path of success. In fact, there is no other option. Having once exhumed the gin, there is no going back. Push ahead and hard. Your dreams will come true.

Life: Many a Splendid Things

What is splendor and is it within our reach? The Oxford dictionary defines it as brilliance, magnificent display or appearance and grandeur. Having been blessed with brains, the human beings are capable of distinguishing their lives by imbibing any or all of these virtuous qualities. No extra efforts are needed for all this. The only necessity is clarity of approach to life in general. A life style of simple living and high thinking is what is needed to help us see the true meaning of splendor. Splendor is not just show off of one's fabulous wealth or personal good looks. It is mind's sublime feeling of satisfaction and fullness. Put to effective use these creative faculties and empower yourself with vision and far-sightedness. Then the exclusive assorted virtuous vibes like magnanimity, fairness, open-mindedness, emotional depth and consciousness will lead to a feeling of abundance in mind. Lucky are those who create a world of splendor not only for themselves but also for others too.

Life is many a splendid things like humility, love, compassion, fellow feeling and universal brotherhood. Dream of it, work for it and enjoy the bliss.

Life: A Hard Task Master

Life is no bed of roses. Easy going minds dream of biggies but end up with dreams only. An approach of continuous struggle is the way out for a glorious innings. Pick up a style of ease and see that nothing comes your way without struggling for it. Beginning from entry in school in childhood, education becomes daunting as one grows. One has to struggle to cross from one stage to another: like High School to Graduation to Professional Qualification followed by successfully qualifying in the Competitive Exam for entry into a high end job. The fact is there is no respite for conscientious hard task masters for self. Struggles continue in varying forms in different contexts from time to time. Survive and make progress we must but have to be vigilant and careful lest the focus gets vitiated and leads to adverse situations.

Struggles laced with sincere targeted efforts reward handsomely provided one is precisely aware of the contours of the target one is aiming at and is ready to struggle determinedly more when what is warranted.

My mother used to say, "Forget about luck. Heroic acts and a determined mind can alter the fate lines on your palm and change your bad luck into good one. Be positive and concentrate on action. Positive acts rid you of the feeling of deprivation and make you free of wants. When in distress, do not stretch your hands before others for favors or pecuniary benefits. When really hard pressed and unable to move forward, seek His blessings only and say, 'Lord Almighty, shower your blessings on everyone. Remember, you are part of everyone.' Her reasoning used to be, you may be blessed along with others even if you personally didn't deserve it this time. Therefore, avoid seeking His favors exclusively for the self. That is being petty minded and self-centered.

Given below are few couplets of Sant Kabir which, in my opinion, sum up the essence of a meaningful, carefree and rewarding journey in this universe.

"Bura jo dekhan mein chala, bura na milya koye, Jo dil khojyea aapnon, mujh se bura na koye"

When I started looking for evil in others, I couldn't find it, but when I did soul-searching, I realized, nobody else was evil like me.

"Kabira khara bazar mein sab ki mange khair, na kahoo se dosti, na kahoo se bair"

Which means; 'surroundings do not matter, why worry for what others do. Our deeds alone determine our future.'

Self-Awareness

Life is nothing if not being aware of one's persona. What distinguishes human beings from other creatures? It is the capability of being in full command of self and be aware of one's idea of life.

Self-Awareness is a big package of attributes comprising of various types of capabilities, qualities and skills essential for sustaining one-self well and with honor in this universe. Specifically, it would mean being aware in depth of one's priorities, goals and level of competence necessary to achieve a distinguishable exalted position in society. For this, one must be in full self-command and be aware of one's strengths, level of general competence, level of shortcomings/weaknesses, if any, and being aware of the various skills/inputs essential for making a mark in life: like adequate educational level, skills and professional competence.

Summing up: it follows, therefore, that self-awareness means (i)being aware of one's strengths and weaknesses, (ii) level of competence required for pushing ahead and (iii) one's capability of making up for shortfalls in one's life-sustaining attributes.

An Ambition

A human life without ambitions can be said to be no life at all. Ambition means a strong desire to achieve something that is compelling enough and is holding. An ambition can also be described as a strong urge to secure what attracts one's inner-self. It then takes the form of a target to be achieved by all means. Once bitten by ambition's bug, one's thought process compels him/her to find out the enabling options followed by efforts to design a concrete action plan. Such a person keeps pushing ahead as planned, hates to look back and feels satisfied only after the target is achieved. Remember, a strong feature of the process ought to be clarity of thought accompanied by a strong and steely resolve to push ahead with confidence. But also, keep a tab on waywardness and the tendency of falling prey to some other seemingly attractive options which could be an un-scrupulous ambition. Check its signals, if any, in initial stages itself lest it overpowers your mind and leads to repentance later.

Life is Love

"Rhiman dhaga prem ka,Mut deejo chatkay, toote se phir yeh na jurey, Jurey to gaanth par jaye"

Rahim Das Khaankhana, one of the Navaratnas in Emperor Akbar's Court.

It conveys, "One should not break the bond of love, for when it breaks, it cannot be tied once again and if tied again, a knot appears."

My limited understanding of this piece of gem says, "Love is pure bliss and is eternal. Maintain its sanctity, nurtured with sublime care it flourishes and blooms and once it is forsaken, it ceases to be its original true."

The Oxford dictionary defines love as "Warm liking or affection for a person, affectionate devotion, God's benevolence towards mankind. Such a vast description makes it the most sought after passion in life.

Love is self-less sacrifice and benevolent affection. True love doesn't entertain any expectation of a reciprocal response. There is no give and take. An attitude of honest commitment is a pre-requisite for love to blossom in the life of both the giver and the recipient.

Love is true love only if it is self-less and caring. It oozes out of one's core depths of heart. There is no place for brain, articulation and pre-meditation in a relationship of love. It is a solemn affection that blossoms into love on its own. Love is not just wishful thoughts. It has to be supported by a willful act of sharing. It is an everlasting phase of fulfillment and eternal happiness for both. There is no show-off at all. When it happens, it just happens on its own and stays in the inner-self of both.

Seekers' love for God for many of His Manifestations is sublime and everlasting. But it happens in the life of those who totally surrender to Him and do not pray for any reward or fulfillment of a wish. Love for Him is His Blessings only for those who deserve it and are granted an opportunity by Him to do so. It is a solemn affair, dignified and completely without any expectation of a reward or fulfillment of a wish.

Serving suffering humanity with an open mind and free will, being honest to one's inner-self and avoiding being smart in dealings with others is also a benign form of love of sorts.

Busy bees like working women and home-makers beware: a solemn devotional rhythm in your heart while handling your daily routine too is a prayer and helps in connecting with Him unwittingly. No religion prescribes a rigid routine of prayers for such virtuous women.

Life is: Conquering the World?

Two old-time couplets go thus:

"Maanti hai Duniya manane wala chahiye"

"Jhukti hai Duniya jhukane wala chahiye"

These couplets convey that the world salutes those who possess a strong will and determination to conquer it. Well a question would be, "Is it so easy to conquer the world? Well, the intent here is not to conquer the world, literally. By conquering one's own ineptitude, lethargy and similar other weaknesses, one can push ahead, come what may. And then vast avenues of growth open up before you. Your hard core endeavor to overcome personal weaknesses opens up a world of great possibilities before you. No problem is too big for a determined mind. The so-called odds wither away no sooner a strong will-power takes command.

It is within the realms of possibilities for each aspirant to mould the circumstances in his/her own favor, wriggle out of insurmountable odds and face the uphill looking task with determination, oneness of mind and clarity of objective.

Once one is free of self-imposed inhibitions and a tendency of indecisiveness, the goal walks down to embrace you. The real debilitating and prohibiting factor is a sense of defeat even before the first step is taken out on the path of struggle and that forces us to stay back. Never feel passive. Remember, *'Asha mein hai jeevan, maran Nirasha mein hai,'* so always be optimistic and hopeful.

Being conscious and aware of one's inner strengths, inherent potential and lingering deep urge for achieving something worthwhile leads to success and glory provided the intent is honest and clean.

For aspiring and determined individuals, conquering the world means throwing away the shackles of lethargy and adopting a steely resolve of pushing ahead under all circumstances. Being Worldly-Wise

Life is Being Worldly Wise

What is being worldly-wise? It means being practical in handling worldly affairs wisely: a mature and balanced approach in dealings with others so as to be seen as a palatable and dependable individual. Being worldly wise means being mature, balanced, practical and non-offensive in dealings with others. Human beings are said to be social animals and being careful in conducting oneself in society is the sine qua non for us. Such an approach makes our social life praiseworthy. It helps avoid hiccups and controversies leading to positive responses all over. This, I believe, is *'Duniya-dari ki soojh boojh-- being worldly wise'*. However, let it not be understood that being carefree attitude isn't desirable. 'Be carefree but be careful'.

Human beings are a very wise lot having been blessed with whims and moods apart from logic and reasoning.

Therefore, while dealing with others, one should be careful to assess others' moods and feelings at that moment. One needs to have a practical approach to keep others in good humor to be able to carry others along, of-course without compromising on fundamentals. Remember, educational competence and professional skills alone are not enough. Being practical and realistic is a basic necessity for smooth sailing in this universe. Which also means; one should be tactful, shrewd, circumspect and sensitive to others' susceptibilities also. One cannot and should not call a spade a spade always. Though truth is an un-questionable virtue and one must endeavor to follow it, yet one may either abstain or not bring it up forcefully when the circumstances demand otherwise. Wait, have patience, truth will prevail ultimately.

Restraint is said to be a virtue at the cost of truth sometimes. Silence is a golden virtue which speaks for itself ultimately. It conveys what you have not said, evokes response from the other side and thus may meet your objective. Don't chirp in when not expected. Assess the mood in the gathering and respond cautiously for your loose talk may lead to impatience in others' mind.

When in a group, don't assume that you are the most intelligent person. Your conduct, facial expressions, gestures and style of communicating are as important as the content and context. Do present your views with due emphasis but in a polite and palatable manner. Be attentive when others especially seniors speak. This will help in understanding them well and also to know their mind and approach.

An intelligent and worldly-wise friend told me once when I was dealing with a shrewd and manipulative peer in work place, "Be practical, avoid confrontation with him and try to keep him in good humor. He is a crook of sorts and if offended, may harm you. Avoid him as far as possible. Do not highlight his/her nefarious actions to others. Protect yourself lest he unleashes his venom on you."

Another friend had his own opinion for dealing with others. He believed," Human beings are shrewd enough and their exterior doesn't match with their interior. Therefore, start and stay with this assumption until the fellow demonstrates that he is trust worthy. I, however, always believed otherwise, "Human beings are basically nice and reliable and one should make a beginning with this assumption. Yet be careful until the other person demonstrates otherwise."Be worldly wise to be happy and successful.

Being a Good Listener v/s a Good Speaker

Listening carefully is an asset of big value. Its relevance and importance consists in picking up ideas from others if found useful and praiseworthy and discarding what is seen to be harmful. Careful listening style helps in various aspects. In work life its role is all the more important. It enables one to pick up good ideas from others to improve/polish one's own style of interacting with others; more so in business meetings, group discussions, conferences and presentations etc. It enables one to copycat the style, mannerism and delivery style of others when their style and content of the talk attracts one's mind, when it is seen to be appreciable and praise-worthy. Also, when the content and delivery style doesn't click with your thoughts and you don't find it worthwhile you again learn a lesson; the lesson to upgrade your own skills and be careful in your delivery style and for framing your talk's contents. The result would be due appreciation/approving nod coming your way.

Careful listening style helps in being careful while interacting with others lest you face negative responses. It also cautions you to be circumspect and careful lest your dealings result in hiccups in life. In difficult situations, it helps you to engage in soul searching with a view to avoid in own talk/dealings what was seen to be reprehensible and damaging in others' talk/interaction.

A good speaking style is an asset of immense value for a good and effective speaker only can carry the audience with him/her. It makes the task easy and helps in being successful in putting forth one's views effectively. It enables one to put forth one's mind convincingly to be able to evince positive response and appreciation. An effective delivery style demands paraphrasing the content with facts and supporting data in proper sequence. The delivery style has to be persuasive and appealing. The content and language must be lucid, free of jargons and high-sounding phrases in order to evince proper response(s). Your ability to carry the audience with you will depend upon your manners and style of delivery. Be attentive and careful to be able to handle the observations/questions of the audience satisfactorily. A good speaker is one who punctuates his/her talk with convincing details of the topic and supplements his/her talk with facts lucidly and effectively.

A good listening and an effective speaking style are complementary to each other. You listen carefully and accumulate wealth of good ideas and when you speak well, you pay back and contribute to common good. The flourishing styles of good listening and good speaking are the sum total and evocative essence of a meaningful life.

Life is Courage and Determination

The Pandemic

Starting in 2019, the Pandemic has been persisting and appearing in deadlier mutations year after year. And science and medicine have not yet succeeded in preventing its deadlier variations or eliminating it altogether. The result is human sufferings, deaths and destruction all over the globe. Of course, scientific and medical research has developed vaccines and medicines which are effective in saving lives but the environment of gloom and despair is visible all around.

Yes, apart from prescribed medication and efforts for immunity building etc., being cautious, exercising self-control and religiously following the guide-lines/advisories issued by the Govt. authorities from time to time is essential.

All the same, I believe, the psychological mental pressure of fear can be handled better with hope and self-confidence. Believe in self, have faith in own inner-strength and natural instinct of fighting the calamity with self-confidence.

'Hope is life; losing heart or giving up is fatalistic. Pushing ahead with self-confidence is the nectar of survival in difficult times.'

"Himmate Mardan, Maddede Khuda"(a proverb in Urdu language)

It conveys, "Pushing ahead with determination is human; it evokes Divine Blessings.

In other words, God blesses those who demonstrate courage of conviction and commitment when face to face with a calamity."

Patience

"Patience is bitter but its fruit is sweet. Patience is the companion of wisdom."

Saint Augustine

"Patience is bearing the burden of life cheerfully."

Bhagwat Purana

A few true examples of courage, self-confidence and commitment to overcome the calamity, witnessed at the time of India's partition in 1947, are narrated below which corroborate the sayings given herein before.

In our town, Isa-Khel, dist. Mianwali in Pakistan, there were riots in Sept. 1947. Apparently, on surface, the communal tension was brought under control when the army took charge but it subsisted internally. There were a few meetings between the community leaders but no reconciliation. The dominant Muslim leaders conveyed," embrace our religion for your survival."

Next morning, there were announcements exhorting Hindus to visit mosques and accept the edict by uttering the 'Kalma' in the presence of Maulvis. The word spread in the Hindu community to follow the edict. I (about 10 then) was asked to escort the family's elder lady (92 then) in the queue. Not willing to do so, I started cribbing about this harsh dictate but the lady tried to console me saying; "you are not alone, the calamity has fallen on the entire community. Standing here is just a time gaining move of community leaders. Wait and see what follows."

Our community leaders were in touch with the authorities for arranging armed army escorts for our migration out from there. And few days later, we were safe in the Refugee Camp at Mianwali (the dist. HQ) from where we boarded the train under escort and safely landed in a refugee camp at Kurukshetra.

Elders' Foresight: our Savior in Calamity

Our elders, the mother and elder brother-in-law's foresighted vision proved to be mine and my elder brother's savior. They decided to send us to school in the camp itself to pursue our studies further instead of pushing us as petty street vendors. The far-sighted vision was path-breaking for both of us, but it meant betting on providence. The dream vision was enabling us to pass Matriculation exam in due course for being eligible for the post of a clerk in a govt dept. The desperate position was the family had no cash or ornaments. All were left behind and each one of us had arrived in three layers of clothing. It's God's providence that we both were able to realize our elders' dream in due course.

Smart and apparently difficult decisions made in difficult times pay long term dividends

The moral of the story; "when facing a calamity, don't succumb to it; be patient, think, work out your strategy and follow it up with appropriate action."

Don't Give Up. Innovate to Overcome Adverse Situation.

Giving up or surrendering to adversities is not human or else this race would not have evolved to where it is today. Human beings have the capability to ponder and think of viable alternatives when facing a hazardous or a challenging situation. This process is evident all over again as society faces due to Covid 19, a challenge, the threat of partial extinction and significant loss of material progress made in eradicating poverty. Not surprising that thanks to unrelenting research, scientific community has met the challenge by discovering viable preventive and treatment options and this demonstrates humans' collective ability to find the physical solutions. However, what is left out is the mental impact this pandemic has had on us all. Times are tough so our decisions have to be resilient and also much better thought out. Good luck to us all!

The Conclusion

"It is better to allow our lives to speak for us than our words"

Mahatma Gandhi

"A long life is not good enough but a good life is long enough"

Benjamin Franklin

Discussing life's innumerable manifestations is an infinite journey. I believe it's advisable for me to conclude saying life is being honest to oneself and to others alike. Restraint and being objective and honest in one's disposition in general particularly in the face of adverse situations is an honest tribute to life. If nothing else, it grants you peace of mind so keenly desired by us all.

Other Meaningful Attributes/Facets of Life

Some of them as an illustration are, Being good listener V/s good speaker, Humility, 'Sewa', Rhythm, Fantasy, Trupti, (Satisfaction), Dreams, Philanthropy, Charity, Passion for life, Nobility, Love and Sacrifice, HIS and Elders Blessings etc. etc.

I stop at it and leave it to dear readers to decode them the way they like it.

CHAPTER 4

FRIENDSHIP: A BLISSFUL PHENOMENON

"Adversity is a crucible in which friendship is tested."

Mahatma Gandhi

"Those friends thou hast, and their adoption tried,
Grapple them to thy soul with hoops of steel."

William Shakespeare

The Oxford dictionary defines friend as a person with whom one is on terms of mutual affection independently of sexual or family love or a helper or a sympathizer.

My understanding tells me, "Friendship doesn't signify mutual affection or helpful attitude only."It is a much bigger phenomenon; a bunch of mutual self-less and sub-lime feelings of trust and affection that binds the two individuals together. It embraces an emotional sense of mutual regards. It is devoid of any feeling of selfishness. Friendship being an act of trust is sustained when the individuals truly believe in it and cherish its value. It is a lasting attachment voluntarily oozing out of two hearts.

There is no quid-pro-quo in friendship. It is said, "A friend in need is a friend indeed;" which means friendship's real test lies in coming to the help of friend when he/she is in need of it. Sacrificing own comforts, providing pecuniary support and being happily available to the friend in difficult and adverse circumstances is the crux of a long-lasting friendly relationship.

True friendship; thy name is selfless affection, genuine love and an honest willingness to ignore one's own interests when warranted in a given situation.

Pretension and formality in dealings is not friendship. It is honey trap of which one should be careful, lest one suffers.

A couplet in Hindi cautions us thus, *"Damini damak rahi ghann mahin, khal ki preeti yatha thir naahin."* which means, like lightening in clouds which is momentary, friendship with a person who is dull and lacks wisdom (a fool) is momentary. Such a relationship is not stable like lightening in the clouds, doesn't meet the fundamental nuance of the relationship. However, one needs to be careful and should asses the IQ level of the individual before initiating any such move, otherwise it may turn out to be a disappointment.

It is said, how the bond of friendship materializes is a mystery. No, it is not so. It happens when there is positive mutual attraction towards each other in the first interaction itself. It is a beginning which blossoms in the due course. It starts taking shape after the two mature minds interact with each other regularly. Such an interaction is a prelude to looking at each other's inherent fundamental nuances of life; one's values, aptitude and general disposition. And after both are satisfied, a final view emerges in the form of mutual trust between the two. After that the mutual trust takes the form of genuine friendship. Only such a relationship is steady leading to mutual respect, confidence and comfort in free exchanges.

All this creates an impression as if the relationship has to pass through a cumbersome process of evaluation, no not the least. Evaluating and assessing is a routine activity in humans' sub-conscious mind. And the final confirmation is provided by an affirmative inner-call. Go ahead after this. Once your mature inner-self has accepted it, there is no going back. Cherish it and let it blossom.

All said and done, I believe, friendship is a celestial bounty available to some who deserve it and value its endless benevolent role in life.

Role of Friendship in Life

That the true friendship is an asset of immense value in life is well known. Quite often, a friend comes to rescue promptly when one is in some difficult situation. It is more so now with the advent of nuclear families and off-springs venturing out in search of greener pastures. The elderly back home and the child in foreign land, both need it more for obvious reasons.

One feels freer in confiding in a friend when caught in some difficult situation. This attitude is borne out of the sure feeling that the bits of advice of a friend are sure to be un-biased and frank. The expectation is that the advice is workable and would be helpful if acted upon. Why? Because one hopes a friend would offer advice keeping in mind one's overall approach and preferences in dealing with the problem at hands.

Friendly advice is always welcome for persons who believe in the inherent meaning of true friendship. Apart from parents and the better-half, only a friend happens to be aware of the depth of dilemma one is face to face with. Quite naturally, his/her views would surely be effective and appropriate for the situation. Sometimes, one feels inclined to share sensitive information with a friend and find out his/her response to reconfirm the validity of one's own views. Depending upon the level of free exchanges and openness in sharing personal information, a friend can be trusted more freely to suggest a way out. In times of odd and disturbing circumstances one can look towards a friend and seek his/her support, whether of physical, financial or advisory nature.

Apart from expectations of sane advice and help, friends are a perennial source of strength; provide a feeling of togetherness and comradeship. Indulging in free exchanges, enjoying together in merry making activities like movies, excursions, hang-outs or other fun activities is enjoyable more with friends. Great time spent in the company of friends provides energy, builds up the morale and boosts our confidence.

One of my worldly-wise friends says, 'times are not same as ours were. Harsh competition, nuclear families and ever-flowing high ambitions have banished the free communicative environment all over. The fear of unknown is influencing the thought process. Lack of self-confidence is another villain.' I am not sure if I can subscribe to such a view. I still believe: genuine and unbiased approach in a human mind is dominant always. One has only to explore it.

Last but not the least, sharing freely and happily is the key word in friendship.

Friendship in Work Life

Friendship is a natural phenomenon and it plays an important role in work life also as it does in personal life. However, the process here is fairly different. There are quite a few steps through which it has to pass before it gets established. Considering, the delicate and more formal environment in work places, the first step would be getting properly acquainted with each other. This will take some time. One shouldn't hurry through it. After having known each other for a reasonable time, the relationship moves to the next important stage; assessing individuals' level of openness in dealings. It is important to be satisfied about this basic enabling trait in two minds. Being satisfied in this behalf is an important confidence-building measure. Friendship can neither be thought of nor can it subsist without mutual trust, openness and an attitude of free and frank exchanges.

The question is how does friendship help in work-place considering the formal nature of relationship there? For overcoming and sharing work related problems, seeking each other's help in resolving sundry work related issues like seeking a friend's help when unable to decipher or correctly interpret a rule/regulation, one can always depend upon a friend. Coming to each other's help in moments of difficulty, providing support, emotional as well physical is expected and appreciated in work-place, when necessary. Also, like in normal life, at a work place too, one is free to indulge in humorous chats/gossips in free time to lighten the work related pressures. Even serious issues may be discussed in confidence without compromising on confidence and security issues. It all depends on the level of mutual trust and willingness to share. The level of mutual confidence would determine the level of exchanges in delicate and formal matters also. All would depend upon the depth of shared emotions.

True friendship is always a big source of strength in work life as it is in personal life. Let's remember, true friendship gets nurtured only when its roots are deep enough.

I believe; the bonanza of true friendship is subject to existence of few critical traits in life; (i) one must be care-free, open-minded and willing to share and confide (ii) be far away from prejudices and fear-complexes, (iii) must be self-confident and be sure of own ability to stand firm on personal valued principles in adverse situations also, (iv) and believe in fair dealings and be devoid of un-known imaginary complexities.

How to cultivate and nurse friendship? The process is quite simple and easy. Start with a belief that the other person is equally open, possesses normal qualities of behavior and is dependable like you. Make sure you are satisfied about his/her general disposition, positive attitude, is open minded and he/she is free of prejudices etc. like you. Be sure about it. Take your time for a reasonable period to know that he/she is trust-worthy. Watch out for signs of smartness in dealings, if any and find out his/her overall attitude in relation to fundamental nuances. Also assess whether his/her general behavior in life is similar to yours and you feel at ease while inter-acting with him/her. Be on a watchful mode for a reasonable period to be sure of the entire process before relaxing your vigil and giving green signal to yourself for there is no going back. Then only start believing and inter-acting freely with him/her.

Given the mutual openness in dealings, friendship is a mesmerizing phenomenon and is blissful for both.

Friendship is a natural instinct. It is not at all difficult to find true friends provided one him/herself believes in being a true friend. Walk down the road of friendship with a sincere and open mind. Do not be swayed by negative emotions. Be careful. Have full faith in him/her in whom you believe and whom you have found to be reciprocal and open-minded like you.

Reciprocity is the essence of friendship for it to be enduring and long lasting.

CHAPTER 5

THE ENABLERS
IN OUR LIFE

Our childhood and primary age is primarily under the influence of mother and other family members, neighborhood and school buddies, and primary school teachers. In adolescence, we tend to pick up values on our own, or under the guidance of family elders and other senior known persons. It is primarily in the grown up age that one starts to know the relevance and feels an urge to pick up values from the lives of other well known persons in society. Thus starts taking a shape in our grown up life the concept of a role model and an influencer.

A Role Model

A role model is said to be a person looked to by others as an example to be imitated.

The society comprises of individuals of varying attributes, competence, unique personal value systems, pursuits, preferences, and priorities and those who are accomplished with such attributes are considered to be role models meaning thereby that one can aim to emulate them in own life. On the other hand, an inquisitive mind, an aspiring individual keen on picking up inspiring values from the laudable attributes of such individuals can be said to be a Seeker.

When the two individuals, a Role Model and a Seeker, happen to interact with each other regularly over a period of time, they tend to know each other's approach to life, preferences and choices. This interaction creates inquisitive vibes in the Seeker's mind and he/she tries to find out sub-consciously the real person behind the face one is in touch with. This happens continuously till the seeker starts believing after due diligence that the other person really is of higher caliber than me, possesses distinct praise worthy qualities of head and heart, is a learned, experienced and dependable person worthy of emulation. Then the Seeker starts considering in mind that this person is truly a role-model for me: the expectation being that I would be benefitted by adopting some or all of his/her valuable qualities of head and heart. Over a period of time, depending upon mutual response between the two persons, the interaction takes the form of a truly meaningful and lasting relationship of high value. This culminates in a hassle free innings between the 'Role Model' and his/her friend, the 'Seeker'.

Why a Role Model?

A question can be whether it is essential to look for a role model in life. A view can be that one need not hanker in this direction and be a solo traveler confident of making own moves as felt necessary. Ultimately, how this attitude will shape up is not difficult to perceive. In this way, one is more likely to get deprived of the benefit of effortless learning from the lives of worthies whose lives are truly inspiring. To help thyself, be a seeker be blessed with and an inquisitive mind and aim to acquire gainful attributes for personal growth and benefit by being in the company of a chosen role model. I personally believe: being a seeker demonstrates one's aptitude of effortless learning of healthy values.

Be cautious and beware: before reaching the ultimate stage of such a relationship, take care to avoid certain pitfalls, such as:-

Do not idolize the chosen person for the relationship has to be between equals.

There is no place for hero-worship notwithstanding the sense of regard and respect in mind for the other person. Remember, the intent of the two is as important as the process and the final outcome.

Do not be misled by emotions and imaginary ambitions. Keep a balance, with your eyes and ears always open. Be discreet, use your thoughtful and judgmental abilities, listen to and follow the inner calls and rumblings within, consult the wise elders and friends, if you feel necessary.

As far as possible, avoid choosing celebrities (Page 3 type) or other sundry famous figures in whom you may have developed a fancy through media exposure. Be circumspect, lest there is some misleading posturing.

Before arriving at an affirmative decision, make sure you know the person well and are sure of his/her laudable attributes.

Don't ever be under the influence of greed lest, in the process, you make a wrong choice.

Remember, the process is as important as the final outcome. Do not be in a hurry. It is said in Hindi, 'Sahejpakey so meethahoey', meaning thereby 'what is cooked slowly (on low flame) is delicious and sweet.'

Keep in mind your ultimate objective, the relationship between the two of you is intended to help you and has to be stable.

The other person would be happy only if you seem to be worthy of his/her company.

What is the Essence of this Relationship?

The foregoing discussions clearly bring out that the role model is the enabler and the seeker is the beneficiary, but the relationship is not based on some pecuniary considerations on either side. It is of sublime nature, is voluntary and its foundation rests on mutual regards. Both the parties are at par emotionally and respect their association. Only then, does the relationship flourish and last longer. The role model is also a party to the process and it is not the seeker only who is keen about it. In my opinion, an important ingredient of the relationship is closeness between the two. It is reasonable to assume that the role model would throw his/her weight behind the proposed relationship and enjoy it if the seeker is seen to be fairly competent and deserving, as also that the seeker's intent is to learn from his/her experiences and ability to help.

It should also be understood that for the relationship to be meaningful, enduring and satisfying to both, regular interaction between the two is its *sine-qua-non*.

Is this Relationship Important?

This relationship is crucial and important because it helps in learning from the experiences of those who:-

(i). have recognizable and meritorious achievements for public good to their credit, and/or

(ii). have put in a lot of efforts and have reached an inspiring and creditworthy position of being an icon in his/her own life,

(iii). have demonstrated in some way a helpful and caring attitude for the needy, are knowledgeable and have full command on their specific subject(s)/ specialization, have been associated with conceiving and successfully implementing important projects/ assignments,

(iv). are well known in society/work-place/office for their singular performance and outstanding results,

(v). possess noble qualities of head and heart,

(vi). are known to be gifted with an amiable personality and one can freely communicate with them and those who have known them earlier appreciate their willing and open attitude in guiding and helping others.

Given above is a narrative list of the commendable virtues only but it would be un-realistic to expect and look for all the virtues in a person before attempting to look up to him/her for the role of an icon.

Considering your own preferences and level of awareness and the field/specialization you have in mind, proceed ahead in building up the relationship with a person you are already acquainted with. Remember, a willing attitude of the person is critical and prior acquaintance with the person is the only way out. Making attempts otherwise is unlikely to be helpful.

For a genuine seeker, association with such a gifted person would prove to be an opportunity of significant consequences. The result of such an association would depend upon how the seeker nurses it, is able to establish his/her credentials of a genuine seeker and is honestly grateful to the role model.

An Influencer

Whom do we call an influencer? The Oxford dictionary describes influence as the 'ability to affect someone's character or beliefs or actions.' Hence, in my opinion, there is no difference between a role model or an influencer except that whereas a role model is a person whom you have known personally, are in regular contact with him/her: an influencer may not be known to you personally and you may not be in direct contact with him/her. The influencer may be a teacher in the school, or just a next-door common man, a leading public figure, an artist, a player, a senior bureaucrat/technocrat, an industrialist or a business man, a professional, a religious figure or even a politician. However, whosoever may be an influencer for you, the primary consideration would be his/her qualities or attributes which attract you and induce you to follow suit.

Following somebody randomly or adopting a cult or a dogma blindly must be avoided. Blind faith or getting swayed by emotions can be highly detrimental and must be avoided. Remember, the influencer you have in mind is neither bothered nor is affected at all. It is you who intends to seek valuable inputs for applying them in your life for your good. Therefore, you must be circumspect in this exercise.

Do not be in hurry to copy-cat others. Apply your judgment to make sure about the validity of the demonstrated values/moves by the person in focus. Let the ideas flow in freely but be cautious.

My personal Experience of Being a Seeker

Let me share a live experience of a Seeker (Me) in finding a role model who initiated me onto the path of this benign relationship and helped me to find my moorings in my work and personal life.

I came into contact with Mr. J.R. Pasricha, my Accounts Officer, when I started my innings as an Auditor in AG, Punjab office in Shimla in 1959. It was my good fortune that he happened to be my Accounts Officer for about four years when I was in the formative age-group of early twenties. The sterling qualities of head and heart that he was blessed with were mesmerizing and evocative. These four years of prime youth spent under his tutelage by a raw and rustic individual like me were truly inspiring. A sincere, dedicated officer, Mr. Pasricha led me by his personal example. He made me realize the importance of being sensitive to my job. His advice, "Be lenient and helpful while finalizing the pension claims of retired personnel" was the beginning of our meaningful relationship. He emphasized, "Providing quick relief to the pensioners by not delaying their Pension Payment Orders must be our focus and we must ensure that this remains our guiding principle." I became enamored of him for his apparently simple looking but actually meaningful attitude as a responsible and compassionate govt. Audit Officer. His genuine commitment to the job assignment matched with that of mine and I felt I was lucky to have met him.

I refrain from elaborating our personal relationship. It would be sufficient to say that he helped enrich the life of a naïve and rustic individual like me. Pasricha family's caring attitude and abundant love helped me to grow and pick up the gentle nuances of life.

Let's remember; a relationship based on tacit love and mutual regard is as important as air and water for life. Nothing needs to be spoken or formally communicated when two individuals reach this high level of shared values.

CHAPTER 6

THE SKILLS OF CONSEQUENCE

Skill has been defined as ability to do something well which means that in addition to general competence, one needs to be proficient in handling skillfully, his/her given assignments satisfactorily. The ability to do justice to a given assignment is an essential additive to one's professional competence to end up as a great performance.

This chapter takes up and discusses skills of pertinent nature which have the potential to add value to one's performance. They streamline one's approach for handling a given assignment to help achieve satisfaction and recognition. The discussions herein are of practical genre and are sure to help streamline one's approach to life: both personal as well as professional.

Communication Skills

The Oxford dictionary describes communication as 'imparting or exchange information', which would mean one's competence and ability to communicate/convey one's mind appropriately with relevance to the subject, topic or issue under consideration; whether in writing or through a word of mouth or appropriate gestures.

Human beings are social animals and the level of depth and proficiency in communicating well with others keeps getting critical as we grow. It is more so when one starts looking for recognition; be it in school/college, competitive interviews or a subsequent stage of seeking and securing a job. The need to communicate effectively is *sine-qua-non* for recognition in every stage of life. In fact, one's future is intimately linked with ability to communicate well; be it in family, school, college or a competitive exam, a work place, vocation, public life, industry or business.

Effective communication skills only can help us succeed whatever be our field of operations. They are of paramount importance throughout our life but are extremely critical for the youngsters who seek recognition and who aspire to make it big in life. Find out whether you are getting positive response when communicating with others. If not satisfied, think of self-help and take help/guidance from professionals. One of the British Prime Ministers, for his own reasons, took to speaking in front of a looking glass with a view to monitoring his communication skills and continued with the process till he was satisfied with his level of performance. That was long back but the inherent message is clear. Beware of the importance of effective communication style. Take advantage of the revolutionary change in communication technology and be happy.

Few Practical Tips for Self-Help

Here is how:-

✓ When making a presentation in a group, make sure the text is lucid, pertinent and crisp. Avoid jargons and high sounding phrases.

✓ Be a great listener. Unless you listen carefully, you would miss to pick up from others the attributes necessary for an effective communication style.

✓ Cultivate the habit of being an attentive listener by choice, take notes and you will be better placed to learn from others and gather some valuable tips.

✓ When in a meeting, observe carefully the delivery style and overall mannerism of the speakers.

✓ Be careful and choosy about your outfit which has to be relevant and impressive for the occasion.

✓ 'Pehle tolo phir bolo.' i.e. weigh before you speak. A few loose words, sentences or phrases may offend others resulting in a missed opportunity or you may be ignored altogether,

✓ Pay attention to your tone and tenor when speaking. Modulate it well so that others listen to you attentively.

✓ Relevant but small sentences and careful paraphrasing of the content draws listeners' attention with obvious message; 'your message has been well-received.'

✓ Make use of idioms, quotes and examples of successful speakers, living or past, to enrich your point of view.

✓ Effective speaking is an art. Take the help of electronic media to learn how to articulate your viewpoint well. Listen attentively to debates and discussions by experts on the radio and TV. Even movies etc. do offer quite a few tips on style, delivery and mannerism of speech. Pick up what appeals to you, practice and make attempts to improve yours.

✓ Rapport building is an effective means for building up and sustaining relationships. Follow others who are proficient in this art to tone up your own ability.

✓ Parting message after a meeting or a gathering is a big help in conveying effectively your final view point. It plays a useful role in emphasizing the essence of your view point. Learn it from others by keen observations if you find you lack this skill.

Observation Skills

"Look on the world with open eyes."

Rabindranath Tagore

"Men are born with two eyes but with one tongue in order that they should see twice as much as they say."

Charles C. Colton

The quotes above of learned icons draw attention to the need for not just looking at but paying close attention to and picking up inherent meanings of what one comes across in daily life. I believe: keeping eyes and ears wide open and straining brains to taking careful note of the deeper meanings of the happenings around is the art called observing.

The Oxford dictionary defines observe as 'perceive, become aware of, watch' which means a habit of not being just aware of but perceiving also. Just looking at others and their responses in a given situation by itself is not enough. One should carefully take meaningful note of the happenings around and the exchanges between individuals or in the groups. The objective being to look at and assess for oneself the underlying ideas behind the interaction with a view to benefit from what was observed: to adopt what seems to be positive and refrain from doing what is seen to be debilitating and not appealing.

Observing others carefully is intended to improving and polishing one's own approach in dealings with others. It provides an intellectual advantage at nobody's cost. On the contrary, just limiting one-self to watching only would mean *status quo* .Such a people miss an opportunity to learn from the likeable experiences of others. Only those with an inquisitive mind do pick up valuable inputs from the life, behavior, style and attitude of others. Be open-minded, welcome new useful ideas to improve your own style.

The knowledge gained in schools/colleges/ professional institutes is a pack of great importance for moving ahead in work-life or in business etc. but is said to be half-way through. This knowledge needs to be polished with practical wisdom which one can supplement with a keen observational attitude. Observational attitude is a step forward in improving and polishing gainfully what we leant in school, college or an institute.

Accumulating healthy lessons is not the only output of keen observational attitude. In the process, one also learns to sift grain from chaff and eliminate negative traits. It is a double whammy; retain positive values and be aware of the negative ones.

Shall we say; observing carefully means coming closer to practical conclusions and drawing own lessons for own benefit out of the acts of others. This skill is free but at the cost of your ability to secure it by careful observational attitude.

Always keep your eyes and ears open. Let fresh ideas flow in. All this is a life-long process. Age is no bar. The more you observe keenly the happenings around you, the wiser you become irrespective of the level of your own wisdom. The beauty is, 'the more you observe, the more you get hungry for accumulating knowledge/wisdom from others' acts of omission and commission'. There is no end to this learning.

Behavioral Skills

The meaning of behavior given in the Oxford dictionary is 'manners, conduct, way of behaving.' Simply put; it means the manner in which we conduct ourselves and behave with others. We all know; our manners, conduct and behavior with others is as important as other important skills. One's mature, dignified and skillful behavior brings in regards, respect and a nice comfortable position in the minds of others. Your behavior demonstrates whether you well deserve to be listened with attention and care. Your nice behavior reflects your sweet will and endears you to others. Remember: being fluent in communicating and being ready with convincing details/data alone is not enough unless it is supplemented by healthy gestures and polite voice modulation.

Let's think of a live work-life example. In business, presentations/negotiations are a necessary routine for finalizing contracts. A bidder is required to present his case before a gathering of decision makers. The result of negotiations will be vastly influenced depending upon the conduct, manners and delivery style of the presenter. Also, one's tone and attitude will add value to the exposition and balance may tilt in your favor if you articulate your views politely but firmly and convincingly.

'Attitude' is a fundamental attribute of behavior. It shapes and gets reflected prominently in our behavior. A balanced and dignified attitude coupled with pleasant manners adds charm to the inter-action; whether in a professional group or otherwise in life. One's attitude influences the surrounding environment one is exposed to. Can it be enriched with personal efforts? The answer is 'Yes' and one should have a re-look and make efforts to enrich it when felt necessary.

The virtuous skills of effective communications and observation are not enough to help us to succeed and grow if our conduct and behavioral style is not persuasive. Persuasion adds value. Even high educational levels, professional competence, ability to conceive and successfully implement projects or for that matter any other field with which one may be concerned, may not yield positive results if we fail the test of acceptable behavior. Also, irrespective of our high level of competence in communication and observation skills, no-body would care for us and offer meaningful co-operation if we fail to impress others in a persuasive manner. Good manners and persuasion in behavior are important for success as any other skill.

A highly damaging attribute in behavior is ego. Ego is the worst possible destroying element. Howsoever, one may be more competent and knowledgeable than others; the inter-action would lead to highly damaging outcome if the behavior and delivery of message/talk is not devoid of ego. Be down to earth practical in dealings with others. Be patient in looking for a response.

Simply put; good behavior and suave manners are not a one-time affair. It is a life-long necessity. Shun ego and be successful.

CHAPTER 7

A HAPPENING LIFE: FEW TIPS FOR

Being Humble; an Honest Call

Banish your ego, care not for self if you want a position/ status for even a seed comes up as a vibrant plant only after being put in dust/earth." What a meaningful call it is. Being humble in life and avoiding high handed attitude in dealings is the essence of a successful innings in the universe.

I am reminded of a poster in my class room in primary school (1941- 1945) namely, "Neki kar darya mein daal." It conveys. 'Perform a noble deed and forget it.' Do not boast after you help somebody or provide succor to a needy person.

An old, my school time couplet, says, "Mun mandir mein gafila, jharoo roz lagaya kar, baith akela do ghari Ishwar key gun gaya kar"

It tells; sweep petty harmful thoughts off your mind daily. Sit down alone for some time in prayers and thanksgiving to HIM to be able to achieve tranquility and peace of mind.

Welcome Your New Day: Be Hopeful

Beware; every new morning is replete with new hopes/ideas waiting for you. Endeavor to capture them. Better be an early morning riser and when up, thank the Lord first thing first. Learn to seek and live by Lord's blessings.

Sit down peacefully with your early morning cup of tea/coffee and let the surging ideas create their magic before you. This is the time for introspection, to plan your day and firm up schedules/activities. Record them in your diary: physical or an electronic aid, as the case maybe. It will be a big help in prioritizing the assignments and scientifically managing your time.

What if you are not an early riser and exigencies of job keep you occupied in work till late in the evenings also? This happens for sure when you are handling higher and bigger responsibilities. The way out is similar. Be your normal self in the morning whenever you get up, pray for few minutes and convey thanks to your Lord for the wonderful gift of sound sleep during the night. Honestly, this prayer session even if of a few minutes will enable you to feel relaxed for long. Get going as you please during the day. At night, before going to bed, again have some pleasant inter-action with the Lord and see you get sound sleep. Off-load the day's burdens and try to keep them off. You will find the new day to be as charming and full of hope as were the previous ones.

Believe me; this routine is not difficult to follow. Yes, the definite requirement is total faith, devotion and honesty of purpose.

Sparing few minutes for a frank communication with the Lord is possible and essential even when you are awfully busy. If nothing else, do it while travelling for and coming back from work. Exigencies and pressures of jobs have trained you to conserve and manage time scientifically. Make use of this skill and spare few moments honestly for an inter-action, even though very small, with Him. Lord knows well your compulsions. But during the week-ends, do spare some time for an inter-action with Him in isolation, which preferably be done in an exclusive place in the house: call it puja/prayers room, as you please. The few minutes spent on this simple routine add to your confidence, make light of your burdens and conveying thanks becomes your normal routine in life. Remember; the additional advantage would be for the lady of the house; take good care of this exclusive place, decorate it well with full devotion and care. Furnish it with items of your choice and keep it tidy and well-maintained.

Health is Wealth: Preserve It

It is said: "Health is Wealth."

"Healthy Mind in a Healthy Body" is another oft quoted verse.

Both are universal truth and mean that a healthy person only can aspire to generate wealth for him/herself and one's mind can be healthy only if one's physical health is sound. In other words, health and wealth are inter-linked. A completely physically fit and mentally alert person only is capable of devoting uninterrupted attention to life's issues and assignments whereas an un-healthy person being worried about his physical fitness is not able to concentrate and devote uninterrupted attention to his/her work.

A healthy person with a healthy mind alone can think rationally and handle life's issues objectively. Planning thoroughly well and making measured moves can be expected of a healthy and mature person. Being pragmatic is yet another attribute of such persons. Healthy persons are not afraid of facing odds. They take them as a challenge and can craft strategies to come out successful. To conceive and plan for future growth is possible only by a healthy mind.

Remember, positive nuances and rational thoughts are feasible only in a healthy mind. Such a person is bestowed with capability to look ahead pragmatically. An out of the box approach and thought germinates only out of a healthy and carefree mind. Such a person is bestowed with capability to look ahead objectively thanks to his/her pragmatic disposition and mature mind. Such persons are not afraid of facing odds/obstacles. They take them as a challenge and can craft strategies to come out successful.

Inspiring and motivating the team, drawing out concrete plans and successfully implementing them is possible only if you are gifted with a healthy and positive thought process.

Those with an ambitious mind and those who aspire to make it big in life must take good care to be fit and alert always. Good health and physical fitness should be your key concern. Neglecting health or indulging in unhealthy practices has its own perils. The choice is obvious and clear.

It is necessary to take care of the need for keeping oneself always physically fit and mentally alert. Be busy in your assignment(s) as warranted by the circumstances but do not ignore or neglect your physical and mental well-being. Keeping fit and alert always must be your key concern. Develop a routine of fitness: a brisk morning walk in an open and clean space. Better if it is a well developed park full of green lawns and healthy environment. Some other options can be exercises, work-out in a Gym, Yoga, meditation and other similar activity as per your choice and liking.

Take good care of yourself and be happy and successful.

Prevention is Better than Cure

We often heard this phrase from our elders whenever we were seen to be landing ourselves into trouble: an illness which was avoidable but for our negligence of ignoring their advice or a physical hurt caused because of our careless attitude and overlooking the requisite precautions or a psychological shock of missing the targets in exam. The underlying message would always pinpoint to our negligent attitude but for which the sorry state could have been prevented. The underlying focus would be on prevention. The emphasis would be on: 'A stitch in time saves nine.'

Dos and Don'ts about food, physical fitness, healthy sleep cycle and similar other preventive measures in general are well-known and if followed with due care, help in preventing regrets later. The target of a healthy and care free life, both personal and work life can be achieved if one prevents oneself of the temptation of being careless. However, it is often argued that today's highly competitive environment doesn't enable the aspiring individuals to follow the discipline rigidly. Travelling extensively, partying and being awake till late night and not being able to rise early is a fact of life for a vast majority of working people. What to do then? To allow the drift to continue unchecked and face the harmful consequences or look out for some 'escape option'; say a well structured routine? I believe, the 'escape option' is the only hope for minimizing the adverse impacts of extremely hectic work life. The scientific time management skills being put to use in work life should get same priority in personal life like any other planned activity. Ignoring self in pursuit of a successful innings in work life is bound to result in physical difficulties later especially in silver years. Take care in time and be happy.

Time: A Precious Commodity

'Time is money.' Is it true? Yes, time is a valuable asset and when well utilized in the right direction and at the right time shows surprising results. It helps in building up resources, liquid as well as physical which are necessary ingredients for sustaining life. If not utilized judiciously, it deprives us of an opportunity of significant consequence. Sincere efforts put in time in the right direction provide a sound lead for success. Growth; thy name is effective time-management. Let's remember, great inventions, scientific discoveries, arts, huge literary wealth and various fine arts wouldn't have been possible if the proponents had not made effective use of time.

An old saying tells us, 'Strike when the iron is hot.' Yet another one says, '*Ab pachtaye kya hot, jab chiryan chug gayin khet.*' It is no use repenting for loss after having missed an opportunity for timely action. Decide instantly when warranted by the prevailing situation and take appropriate action instantly. Delay may mean loss of a significant opportunity or result in embarrassment and/ or pecuniary loss or both. Wavering mind and inaptitude are signs of incompetence. One has to be guided instantly and decisively by the long term impact of the postponement or delay. Postponing it in the hope that time will present an optimum opportunity later is a fallacy of which one should be careful. Decide firmly in time and face the emerging situation calmly with confidence. A delayed decision may result in a difficult and harsh outcome coping up with which could be near impossible. Why cry over spilt milk? Seize the opportunity in time, strike and be rewarded. Else the result would be nothing else but repentance.

For discerning individuals, time well utilized has the potential of showing astonishing results. Only wise people make judicious use of this valuable asset and keep pushing higher and higher. Sound principles of effective time management call for its timely utilization in avenues of choice.

Effective time management is an essential concept of consequence. Its relevance for implementation of projects in time is being emphasized even in Govt. departments nowadays like the corporate world, businesses and industry circles. The common refrain is, 'there is no space for slippages, time over-runs or cost over-runs. Projects must be completed in time and within the allocated resources. Competition, nay, survival itself makes it imperative for the incumbents everywhere to listen to and practice this 'Mantra.'

To conclude: "Time is a precious asset and essence of life."

Securing Future: As Important As Life Itself

Giving thought to plans for future is as important as was your approach for securing a job of choice and liking or venturing into a commercial project of your choice. The success you achieved in your efforts in this behalf is a well-deserved compliment of which one can and should be proud of. However, after thus being successful one tends to give a leeway to oneself. Well, I would say it is quite a natural instinct. After all, savoring hard earned money and basking in the glory of fame is human. But be careful and shun the tendency to splurge. *"Take care of pennies; pounds will take care of themselves."*

However, what is equally important is paying attention to life after retirement from job or the venture you created and established successfully. That calls for monetary planning for future needs in a manner which would ensure meeting your obligations of healthy and a comfortable life for both of you. The assumption here is that you have successfully met the obligations of children's education and related responsibilities of helping them for job or a venture, and creating a living accommodation for family and related necessities like a vehicle(s) etc.

An Attitude of Careful Time Management:

Attitude means a way of thinking or behaving. The relevance and importance of developing an attitude of effective time management is all the more important for the aspiring individuals. In fact, in the present day of highly competitive scenario, it is being emphasized and practiced from school level onwards itself.

In common parlance, it is often said:-

'Time and tide wait for no man',

'Time is always on the side of those who will wait upon it',

'Time is a circus, always packing and moving away.'

The few above old sayings of wise men convey how important time is in one's life. The ambitious souls are careful in handling and putting to use this precious commodity diligently and achieve something worthwhile in life. The others who don't care to heed the sane voices of elders yield nothing but regrets and jealousy only.

Progress or growth is the cherished target of all. But not many care to pick up a lesson or two from the growth stories of those who made it big in life by effective, planned utilization of time and by not squandering off this precious commodity.

Is it we don't care thinking the time is freely available? True, it is available but is precious because time is the basic input for converting opportunities into success stories. How does one utilize time is the crux of one's story. The result will be either satisfaction and glory or despair and regret depending upon the graph and trajectory of its utilization.

I believe: time is money; nay a virtual gold mine and is an asset of immense value. If utilized effectively, it brings forth pleasant surprises. Time well-managed and gainfully utilized is the base on which each individual's graph of life swings. When utilized well, it yields dividends much beyond expectations.

It is said, *'gaya waqt phir haath aatta nahin'* which means time once lost is opportunity lost forever. Strike in time and enjoy the bliss of full satisfaction. However, let's understand, time alone will not yield results if it is not accompanied by the other critical inputs like solemn commitment to the goal/objective, matching hard work, a determined mind and an enthusiastic approach though time is one of the most important factor in the process.

Character and Life: Intertwined?

"Upon ages of struggle, a character is built."

"Character has to be established through a thousand stumbles."

Swami Vivekananda

"Character is like a tree and reputation like its shadow.

The shadow is what we think of it; the tree is the real thing."

Abraham Lincoln

Is one's character same as life itself? Yes, character is the sum-total of values of an individual's conduct in life. A praise-worthy character can be built only after long strenuous struggles.

One's character defines and highlights one's back-ground, heredity and morals. A healthy character is a foundation upon which rests on one's reputation. We faulter when we hanker after our reputation ignoring the base, the foundation..

The Oxford dictionary defines character as 'distinguishing quality; mental or moral qualities, reputation; odd or eccentric person.' We can say; one's character reflects and shapes one's thoughts and conduct. In fact, it reflects completely on our persona and our existence in totality as a human being. Therefore, if we value life and its manifold charms, we must not only cultivate and adopt sound principles of not only character building but also aim to guard against the breaches and decline of values in life. Be careful, the temptation to ignore the sound principles is always anxiously waiting in the wings to seek entry into your mind. Guard against adopting or falling prey to degrading values. After all, what is life if it is shallow and devoid of sound principles of character building? Avoid harmful rat race. Live for what you believe in.

It is rightly said, "If wealth is lost, nothing is lost. If health is lost, something is lost. But if character is lost, everything is lost."You not only lose self respect and face self humiliation but are also subject to serious and degradable rumblings within. One also suffers the ignominy of ill reputation. The society also looks at you with suspicion. A step further could mean you have forfeited the right to live honorably. The society will decide its course of relationship with you accordingly. Do not lose heart. Be optimistic and believe in your inner strength. It is possible to make amends with sincere hard efforts and right approach.

On the contrary, a sound, praise worthy character leaves behind a trail of healthy values and motivates others to follow suit. Even if you are in a small minority in this endeavor, let it be so. Sooner or later, the society will recognize your worth and accord a position of recognition and respect to you. In any case, your progeny will be highly motivated and feel proud of you. Leave behind a legacy of honorable position and laudable legendary character for them to follow.

PART II

WORK LIFE: CHALLENGES AND OPPORTUNITIES

Idea of Success: A Compelling Force for Crazy Minds

The idea of success means an urge to secure success in one's endeavors under all circumstances, favorable or challenging alike. It means the culmination of a well-conceived plan and its successful execution. Without such an approach, success remains confined to brain as a wishful thinking only. One is entitled to feel happy and satisfied only after the plan is successful.

Success knows no limits. Success is life's elixir when earned through honest hard-work. Only great performances lead to success; wishing only does not. An old wise saying proclaims, 'If wishes were horses, beggars would ride.' Be practical. No day-dreaming. Wishing per-se is a welcome first step since no wish means no urge for being creative. Well, just making a wish (vow) is not enough. Rise to the occasion and put in appropriate and matching efforts through hard work and sincere commitment. You would see, success is waiting at your doorstep. Such a success is bliss, a perennial stream of glory. Yes, success intoxicates some wayward individuals but stimulates positively the committed ones. Make a choice; be wayward, get intoxicated and lose balance or get stimulated and pick up threads of greater energy to utilize them further in creative activities.

Success motivates and provides enthusiasm for next effort/target. It is a stimulant of high voltage. The more you succeed the more you dream to conquer still higher peaks. Success shines and reflects as a glow on your face. True success abhors short-cuts or half-hearted attempts. Be prepared to neglect yourself, put off your mind from comforts and cozy atmosphere during the phase of struggles. Results will surprise you.

On the contrary, failure is a stigma, is a curse. Remember; you have been blessed in many ways; birth as a human being and being blessed with a brain. Utilize the services of brain positively to your advantage. Success will be within your reach provided you scratch your head and throw away the gin of unknown fear of failure.

A citation in one of the winner's trophies of Anushree, my grand-daughter, proclaims, 'Go ahead, Stay ahead, and Keep your head.' Could there be a more meaningful lesson for budding aspirants like her? It is God's grace that she knows the deeper meanings of this citation and is well set in her journey of struggles for achieving greater heights in different spheres of her education.

A few thought provoking practical tips picked up by me from the Wall Street Journal from an article of Mr. Charles T Munger, an associate of Mr. Warren Buffet, a legendry Billionaire and Philanthropist.

"If you stay rational yourself, the stupidity of the world helps you."

"I think; we have had a temperamental advantage: Warren and I know better than most people what we know and what we don't know. That's even better than having a lot extra IQ points."

"People chronically miss-appraise the depth of their own knowledge that it is one of the most basic parts of human nature. Knowing the edge of the circle of your competence is one of the most difficult things for human beings to do. Knowing what you don't know is much more useful than being brilliant."

Knowing self fully well is the key for success in life. Success cannot be achieved without firm action, grit and gumption. Work hard to acquire these sterling attributes. Pursuing success is no child's play. It appears to be far away until you achieve it. However, when achieved, success multiplies in the form of abundant joys, breeds satisfaction and enthuses us to seek more. It adds meaning and charm to life. It is like tasting blood, as they call it. It opens up gushing streams of positive energy, broadens one's vision and leads to enthusiasm in handling the affairs of life. Success knows no boundaries. Depending upon one's attitude and expectations, it may sometime seem to be momentary and finite but its impact is always positive.

Be humble and make sure success doesn't enter into your head and puts you off. Being humble after an episode of success is a virtue par excellence. Don't let an episode of success overwhelm you and intoxicate you for that would be a sure recipe for slide down. Be careful and guard against it. Such an approach keeps pushing ahead and helps in repeating new and bigger tales of success. Also remember ill-founded jealousy and arrogance may crop up. Be careful and keep a check.

Do not start singing paeans to your success for it would lead to a sense of lull and kill the urge to keep pushing ahead. In fact, humility is the twin sister of success. Even a small step forward is an encouraging trigger. Make use of it as a stepping stone for still bigger aims. Refrain from show-off after an episode of success. Take success into your strides. It will help in repeating new and bigger tales of success.

Let's remember; success brings in its wake great responsibilities too. Be ready to handle them with equanimity. My mother used to say, "Neither gloat nor indulge in show-off. Be balanced and normal. True success has its own eternal trail of mesmerizing glory. Conserve it."

Few more thought provoking practical tips picked up by me from Wall Street Journal dated 4/10/2014.

"To succeed, don't pick a hero. Figure out your own tendencies, play up your strengths and be aware of your weaknesses. You may have the vision, but you also need the input of others. Look for people who complement your strength, not just ones who compliment you.

Building a team isn't enough: distribute the credit and the spoils.

Don't forget to share your success.

Make your strategy as compelling as your mission. Innovation is not enough; you also need strong implementation to deliver on your ideas.

If you aren't comfortable getting outside your head, surround yourself with people who are."

Linda Rotenberg

My understanding of this brilliant exposition tells me, 'believe in self and your inner strength.' However, in case, you are not comfortable with your conceptual ideas and thoughts, look out for people who you think are. Build up a team of competent people who are clear headed and add value to your thoughts but not the ones who just appreciate you. After having built up a team of choice, keep aside your personal plans and your personal strategy for execution. Re-work out the plans and their execution strategy by including inputs of other members of the team. Make sure, the final strategy and its execution is strong enough and is in line with your concept and thoughts you and your team had conceived. After having successfully executed the project, do not ignore to complement your team and make sure to share the credit and rewards with team members.

"Why aim for less? Think and work for meteoric rise, celebrity status (not of page 3 type), position of genuine respect and admiration in society and much more. No hurdle is too big. Push yourself to be a role model for others. The recent glorious success of Mr. Modi as the Prime Minister of world's biggest democracy, India, is there for everyone to see. Coming from humble origin, he has made it to the top as a democratically elected leader with thumping majority in Lok Sabha."

- (Excerpts from an article by Linda Rottenberg in Wall Street Journal04/10/2014}

"To be successful, you have to be selfish, or you may never achieve. And once you get to your highest level, then you have to be un-selfish. Stay reachable. Stay in touch. Don't isolate."

Michael Jordan

In my view, the iconic message of this wise piece is, 'be self-centered and get isolated while chasing your dreams, be single-mindedly focused on your aim only. When you reach the pinnacle of success, come back in society and be your normal self again.'

Take up one idea.

Think of it, dream of it, live on that idea, and just leave other idea alone."

Remember, the urge for success occurs in mind when you are crazy about it; you constantly give thought to it and single-mindedly give a workable shape to it.

Given below are the three Gs which I believe most of you may be well-conversant with them already. But I can't stop myself from bringing them up here for this trio-sum meant to me a deep practical philosophy of life in general where:-

Grit is Endurance,

Gumption is Common Sense, Resourcefulness, and Enterprise

Gut means Force of Character

A simple reading of the meanings given above are compelling enough for the hopefuls; hopefuls who are chasing success in their endeavors. They provide deep insight into how inspiring these 3 Gs are. Adopt them, capture the deep meanings behind the meanings given in the dictionary and find you have found a way out for chasing success meaningfully. Making attempts to pursue success without being motivated by the positive and affirmative lead in mind is sure to be disappointing.

Success - A Universal Human Urge

The Oxford dictionary defines success as a 'favorable outcome; doing what was desired or attempted, the attainment of wealth, fame or position.' It's too broad a spectrum but quite meaningful and refers to success as a positive trait of mind only. It excludes negative and harmful traits and rightly so for success in achieving what is debilitating and negative cannot be said to be an urge for success. Success when achieved with the help of deception, fraud, ill- will and similar other negative means is no success. A clean and an open mind is the prerequisite for categorizing success as success. Just for an illustration; can a huge mansion or a palace built up with the help of toil of poor laborers be termed as success if the work-force was denied their rightful wages and facilities?

Success is an inner feeling of happiness after achieving what was planned. It brings in satisfaction and prods one to keep pushing. The first instance of success gives impetus to the urge for doing and achieving more and more. It's a positive and compelling force for the ambitious souls. Success stimulates and provides fodder for growth of creative and purposeful streams of thoughts. Success is celebration of one's creativity of thoughts if it gives rise to positive urges in mind. Be careful; lest the negative tendencies overtake and then the success becomes a spoiler and harmful.

Success is the ultimate measure of one's longings for a unique identity: the identity of a hard core distinct performer and possibly a crusader too. However; in general, people loosely talk of success as something just desirable. No, for seriously committed individuals it is a deep-rooted urge for securing for self an enviable position of a successful performer and a leading crusader. However, one has to be sure and determined in the first place what success means for him/her. What is my aim and objective in life and what needs to be done to be successful in achieving what is close to my heart? Let's remember; means are as important as the desired outcome. Those who understand the true significance and relevance of an honest approach can only aspire to secure success and hope to earn the bliss of a meaningful life.

I believe; success is a universal urge and it is meaningful only if it is designed to bring about happiness in life. And the attempt to secure it doesn't get deflected by adverse situations. The act for achieving it is supported by a strong urge for achieving it. And above all, it is not a half-hearted attempt. Remember; adversities do crop up sometime. One has to face them head on with a strong determination.

Remember: wishing only is not enough. A concrete action plan needs to be put in place followed by a detailed execution strategy.

Success loves to be chased by strong, determined and powerful enthusiasts.

The First Significant Achievement in Life

First episode of significant achievement should not be taken as success or a big celebratory affair. Remember, it's just the first step on the ladder. The ultimate aim is far away in the horizon. The day one feels satisfied, the tendency to relax overtakes and the urge for achieving more vanishes. Therefore, keep pushing, do not relent and try to find out the weak spots in your journey so far. The quest for glory and more stimulates those who take the first dose of success as just a beginning. The hunger for doing more pushes them into the arena of action again and again. No doubt, the first step on the ladder of success is a stimulating booster dose of great significance. Keep pushing and chase the bigger dreams with enthusiasm and energy. Celebrate it by all means but do not gloat over it. Recall the stories of success of luminaries who inspire you and you will find they didn't stop pushing ahead till they reached the glorious top.

Apparitional Attitude and Self Confidence

Apparition means something remarkable or unexpected and attitude means a way of thinking or behaving. Put together, apparition and attitude would mean a remarkable and unexpected thought process and self-confidence means pushing ahead with conviction. It follows, therefore, that when an individual is led by a remarkable and uncommon thinking and is pushed ahead with a sense of self-confidence, the result would be extraordinary success. In other words, the deadly combination of apparitional attitude and self-confidence is the ultimate trigger and booster for achieving what one aims at. However, this sense of combining apparition with self-confidence lies dormant till a person wakes up to the need to excel either of his own volition or gets motivated by a lead provided by a well-wishing senior.

We are told, human beings are ambitious by birth but only a few are conscious of it. But it is also true that ambition like other emotions doesn't propel of its own volition. One has to realize it and help it manifest itself as an important urge in one's inner-self. Only then an ambitious mind prodded by self-confidence can beat the obstacles and meet the challenges. But not many achieve what they aspire for because of lack of self-confidence.

Self motivation and well-meaning style of following worthy seniors in home, society at large and work place are also the most effective triggers for picking up important leads and making life worthwhile. Such an approach is a sure trigger for realizing one's dreams. Many of us start dreaming of an enviable position and success but such dreams remain dreams in mind only till a shake-up happens and one is woken up to the importance of being a real performer in life. Who doesn't wish to be a rising star committed to achieving an exalted position in society? Leave behind complacency and push ahead with the duo. That is the essence of a successful life.

The conclusion: Do aspire for growth and success. It is human beings' Magna-Charta of success. Let the gin of ambitions take over. Be positive and hopeful. Let the gin grow on its own. Give it a free hand. You will be surprised in the process when the results overwhelm you.

Beware, only positive ambitions motivate, cajole and lead us in our quest for growth. Believe in self, unleash your potential, put in your best and see success is at your door-step. Care not for hurdles and other negatives in the horizon. Hard dedicated work speaks for itself.

My Experience

After I, a migrant refugee from Pakistan in Sept. 1947, was successful in passing the High School exam, I didn't relent because the first important target of securing a regular govt. job was still far away. I realized that this could be possible only after I overcame my weaknesses; poor English language vocabulary and poor communication skills. I worked hard in different ways to get rid of these weaknesses and ultimately I succeeded in securing the job of a Goods Clerk in the Railways: a first achievement of sorts for a poor refugee boy.

Being a hapless refugee in your own country is the biggest curse in life but making serious attempts to leave behind its debilitating and frustrating impact is a great positive step forward. To be honest, I was thrilled on making a hard earned beginning of significance in life. This significant first dose of success motivated me to further my bigger aims with bigger zeal and confidence. The ultimate step for further regular growth was my success (after about 16 years of struggles and growth in different capacities)in selection as an Accounts Executive in Bokaro Steel Ltd. That was the beginning of a cherished carrier of stimulating growth.

It was then I thought that I had arrived.

Lastly I would say:

I was lucky: the phrase 'honesty of purpose', a mantra given to me by one of my senior uncles not only guided me in my endeavors but also widened my horizon. To me, it meant integrity and sensitiveness in dealings, service with a smile, unbiased and open mind, high performance focused on the end result and no hidden agenda behind any act.Love thy profession and love thy job to have job and personal satisfaction both. Remember: consistent good performance and hard sincere work is appreciated and rewarded on merit Do not entertain any misgivings about fairness in judgment of seniors. Perform with zeal and conviction. Give your best to the assigned responsibility honestly and objectively. Forget about fears of discrimination or victimization.

CHAPTER 2

CHASING SUCCESS

To chase means to push ahead, to focus on the strategy of success and to persist with efforts till success is achieved. The Oxford dictionary says, "Chasing means going quickly after an idea in order to capture and overtake it." And when the idea is to push for success in an endeavor, it overtakes all other ideas.

Given below are some strategic and positive inputs which once internalized keep pushing ahead one's urge for chasing success.

Commitment and Zeal

Commitment means an obligation or pledge and zeal means enthusiasm; hearty and persistent effort. It is said a life is deficient if it is not full of commitment and enthusiasm. Combined together, the powerful duo of commitment and zeal is a potential solemn energy which is capable of overcoming and leaving behind the obstacles, if any, in your pursuit of achieving success. All this leads us to the conclusion that for being successful, an honest commitment and zeal for completing the assignment are as essential as air and water for sustaining life. Just wishing for success without putting our head and heart into it is meaningless and is wastage of resources including the time spent on it. Devote your 100 % with solemn commitment, devotion and energy zealously. The outcome will surprise you beyond your expectations.

Honesty of Purpose

Being honest means truthful, trustworthy and purpose means an intended result, something for which effort is being made, an intention to act, determination. The phrase conveys that for successful execution of a job/ assignment, an honest, trustworthy and dependable approach is essential. Without such an approach, success of the project/assignment may not be possible. In fact, without an honest and truthful bent of mind and without being aware of the objective of the assignment, venturing out is fraught with risks of failure and/or delay. Also, before the responsibility for execution is assigned to an individual or the group, the individual/group should be made conversant with the contours of the proposed assignment. It will help build up trust and confidence between the Management and the individual/team and push the individual/group to complete the job with determination. The key factors for successful execution/ delivery of the results are honest commitment, sharing and mutual trust. In fact, it is mutually beneficial for the Management and the employees to be open in mutual dealings.

It is also said honesty is the best policy. This policy when adopted in life; personal as well as business/work, brings up happy surprises. It has the unlimited potential of enriching life in abundance too

Devotion

Devotion means great love or loyalty.

"Devotion is not difficult. All it needs is simplicity and contentment."

Ramayana

The above two iconic versions/meanings straight away convey that being loyal and devoted in life is a virtue par-excellence. As a general approach to affairs of life, devotion calls for being contented and simple. When devotion is the hallmark of an individual, it is sure to result in SUCCESS of the assignments before him/her, whether personal or job.

Target Setting: The First Crucial Step

Target has been defined as 'an objective', 'a minimum result aimed at', 'to plan or schedule (a thing) so as to attain an objective'. Which means, that for being able to achieve the result one is aiming at, one has to have an objective, a definite plan or a schedule in focus? In other words, a definite target is a pre-requisite for being successful in accomplishing what one seeks to. Some people say target setting is an art while others say it is a challenge. No, it is neither. Let's not get bogged down in jargons. Target setting is just a normal routine but an essential exercise. It helps in keeping in focus the end result that is expected out of the efforts we make for it.

Generally speaking, being successful in life is the common refrain of all human beings. In a broad sense, therefore, 'being successful in life' is the target/aim we all look forward to.

Importance of Targets

To be successful in work life, one is expected to design in a scientific manner the structure of efforts necessary for accomplishing the assignment on hand. And scientific approach demands that one proceeds in an organized way with requisite minute details in the right direction that would help in moving ahead. This exercise would necessitate setting of targets for each segment of the structure separately. When completed, this exercise will keep us glued to the mission and provide a broad frame work of priorities to help us remain focused on the ultimate target; Success. Then helped by strong will power and determination, one moves ahead with a resolve; 'come what may, I will stay on course, will achieve the target and shall not get deterred by obstacles'.

Target setting is a normal activity, a first affirmative step forward for pushing us on to the path of success. It is not a onetime act. In fact, the habit of setting targets is essential even for mundane activities of daily life. Therefore, every time, while thinking of success and planning for growth in work-life, start with the first step-setting of targets of time frame for completion of the assignments and resources required: men, material and services. And if the assignment/project is large involving many activities or sub-activities, setting of the target of completion of each segment separately is necessary.

Reduce the targets in writing or in Project details so as to serve as a guide and reminder for corrective action, when needed. Make sure: the target is neither too rigid nor too high which is sure to lead to an impractical or an absurd approach.

The seniors, who normally set targets, have to keep in the mind the acceptability factor. Better, take the Executives and Staff into confidence, listen to them, keep in mind their suggestions and then take a final view. Unilateral decisions usually lead to differences resulting in negative outcome.

Targets perform the role of a hard task master by implication and keep us aware of the goal. Target brings in its toe *control and discipline* which prod us to act and perform our act in time and as planned failing which the target would remain in our mind or in our diary or in whatever form, always reminding us of our failure/neglect. Its' another important off-shoot is *focus* which is a key tool for making a success of our efforts. It helps in accomplishing within the prescribed time frame and within the approved monetary resources that were planned.

Failure to develop a routine of setting targets would result in lack of control, discipline and focus, resulting in chaos and delay in completion of the project/assignment as planned.

Setting of Targets in Personal Life

An aimless life is shallow, is a drag and a waste of resources. In Hindi, we call such a life *'dishaheen'*, an aimless person. An Urdu couplet amply describes it as 'Subah hoti hai, sham hoti hai, zindagi bus youn hi tamaam hoti hai.' Days and nights spent aimlessly lead to aim-less existence and one reaches nowhere.

The first step is to determine one's aim and objective of life as such. This is the first important starting point in life. Having firmed up after due self-churning the purpose of life, one is expected to be aware in general about one's aim and purpose of life. After it, one needs to formalize the steps that would be necessary for pushing ahead as desired.

Targets are the real task masters and irrespective of the nature and contours of the desired aim, one has to start with setting of targets for each level of activity. Targets bring in regularity, discipline and punctuality in life. Targets goad, make individuals conscious of their role, responsibility to be able to achieve the desired outcome. A creeping but important benefit of being responsible and disciplined flows out of target setting exercise.

When the target is achieved successfully, it yields a serene sense of fulfillment and boosts self-confidence. Another creeping but critical advantage is awareness about the purpose of life. Well, in my opinion, this is the ultimate achievement for any conscious individual.

Targets also play an important role in bringing in discipline. Let's start with childhood. That the child must get up in time, get ready after bath, breakfast and be ready to board the school bus or other means for reaching the school in time. There is dual advantage in this exercise; not only the child learns to be punctual but the parents too learn to be conscious of their role: help and guide the progeny. Well, what can be more important for both at this stage?

Just for example, let's talk of another simple, routine activity. It could be losing weight which is quite common now-a-days. One may be serious about it but results would accrue only if there is a time-bound target and the regime of dos and don'ts is fixed. Similarly, setting of target would be necessary for meeting goals that we may feel are essential for regulating our life.

There is no escape. In fact, setting of targets continues throughout our life in one form or the other. It is a call that we have to take for giving a meaning to our existence.

The setting of targets is the first step for being successful, happy and scoring high on the ladder of success. Therefore, spending quality time on fixing target is essential for making a mark and leaving our unique imprint in each activity of our life. Aim high, dream big, plan and look carefully at various activities thought to be essential for success but do the first thing first; fix targets in details for each segment/component. Great achievements, high position, good name and fame in society become elusive if we do not bind ourselves by the discipline of fixing targets.

Gradually fixing targets would develop as a reflex acting on its own and pushing us for being disciplined in all spheres of life.

Setting of Targets for Entry into a Profession of Choice

The first pre-requisite for chasing dreams of entry in a profession of one's liking is identifying the appropriate stream of education necessary for it. In fact, at school stage itself the targets for acquiring competence in relevant education stream start assuming a critical role. Pick out the stream which is the stepping stone for the profession of choice. Prepare well to be able to enter a college of repute and high standing. This stage i.e. trying to seek entry into a College/University of repute also demands setting of targets for being definitely successful in securing admission. If one fails to do so, a phase of struggles and running from pillar to post begins. Therefore, rigid targets here too are essential. One cannot take it easy and still hope to be successful.At each stage in school and college, one has to fix targets, pursue them with determination and then only one can dream of achieving the goal of beating the competition happily.

Having successfully passed out of the professional college, one is face to face with big question. How to secure a job of choice in an organization of repute? Now is the phase of being extra cautious. It demands a high level of precision in planning and a scientific approach in determining the inputs necessary for success in the IQ process and face-off with the Selection Board. It is altogether a different cup of tea. In practical terms, the first step would be determining the professional competence necessary for the job, followed by study of specifics like competition, environment in the job market, and practical inputs to be provided by professional counselors for success in the selection process. The higher the aspirations, the higher would be the level of preparatory work. All these specifics would be the determinants for fixing of target for each segment separately.

Target Setting: A Continuous Crucial Necessity

Life is a continuous journey and as a quid-pro-quo, it calls for reviewing and setting of targets constantly; the purpose being updating of self in sync with the emerging demands/situations. For example, when one enters a new job, a fresh wave of target setting would emerge calling for allocation of resources, physical and monetary both.

Setting of targets is no big deal. You have been doing so happily since your school days. It is a routine activity for you now but an instructive habit for you.

The beauty in human life is that the drill of setting targets doesn't end with completing the innings of job life. Hereafter, fresh waves of different hues of responsibilities would emerge calling for action based on the targets envisaged for each occasion. Surely, the setting of targets is a life-long affair to help us achieve success at each stage of our journey.

Success follows those who believe in setting targets for each important activity of life, who know the importance of being disciplined in setting of targets in time, who develop focus and work with precision while setting targets, and who understand that without targets one cannot develop vision for meeting the targets and coming out successful.

Targets show us the way for achieving what we believe in and what is our aim of life. Targets are a guide, a vital help and our companion in our struggles. Make friends with them and see miracles happen.

The innocuous target may appear to be a simple step but the real magnitude of the inherent problem may be vast. Therefore, while fixing a target, one has to keep in mind and remember passionately the ultimate goal.

The moral: develop the habit of setting targets as a routine habit to usher in control, discipline and focus in life. Keep in mind the ultimate aim and its various segments. Fix the target in steps if called for and plan the strategy of success accordingly.

CHAPTER 3

FOCUSSED APPROACH: AN ABSOLUTE NECESSITY

Meaning of a Meaningful Work Life

What is meaningful work-life and how it impacts our future? A simple meaning is; understand the purpose for which you are in job. Is it just to earn your livelihood? Or it has some deeper meanings also? I believe: meaningful work life means, being happy only after delivering your best not only to your own satisfaction but also completing the assignment as warranted by your job profile. Make sure it fulfills the objective of the role assigned to you and earns peace of mind for you as well as your employer at the end of the day, every day. Repeat it continuously and let it not be seen as a show-off for a limited period. In the process, who knows, you may become the envy of many? Enjoy being an eye-sore for the non-performers, but diligently only, lest you earn their ire. Don't antagonize such people. Be circumspect in your dealings with them. Don't be seen as a tool in the hands of Management. Maintain your independence and shun any temptation behind any such move.

Not only perform well but also innovate and add value to your role/assignment. Strive not to carry problems, if any, to seniors. Find out what is the end result expected from the assignment you are handling and perform accordingly. Do not expect laurels immediately after a great performance. Be patient and let the big outcome speak for itself. It is also important that you are seen keeping focus on conserving resources being used in the process.

As you move up the ladder, demonstrate you are a crusader, a meaningful leader wanting to lead the team with your skillful aptitude and competence. Do demonstrate; you highly value the confidence reposed in you by the Management. Strive hard to earn the sobriquet of a great leader and an able manager.

My Approach

When I was to leave my house first time to take up job in Indian Railways, my mother advised; "Ascertain and assess the essential contours of your job profile as a first step. Having done so, keep pushing your-self hard to complete the assignment(s) satisfactorily and continuously." Needless to say, I followed it religiously throughout my career. I say, I am happy I did it.

And later, in the course of my work life journey, one of my well-wishing senior colleagues advised me to expand this learning further, as given below. This important advice alerted me and guided me throughout my career. It enriched and added depth to my approach.

It goaded me to look for and work on new ideas for further improvement. "Be your own judge and a hard task master lest you fall into slumber or start gloating."

"Make sure your high degree performance gets the attention of your seniors. It is also important to be noticed and be recognized as a serious performer by your seniors. Understand; it is the only way forward. You must deliver always but make sure you are seen to be doing that."

- Mr. Jagjit Rai Wadhawan, my neighbor and colleague in Shimla.

I picked it up seriously *("Gaanth bandh li"*, as we call it in Hindi) and tried to follow it throughout my career. Honestly, this piece of pertinent advice turned out to be a game-changer for me in my entire work-life.

S.W.O.T Analysis

The technique of SWOT analysis is applied to find out the viability of an expenditure/investment proposal before it is approved and a go ahead is given by the competent authority.SWOT stands for strengths, weaknesses, opportunities and threats. Before taking an investment decision for implementation of high value projects having long gestation periods, the project's viability has to be ascertained. And for this purpose a scientific analysis, called SWOT analysis of the project is done. The project is approved for implementation only if the analysis confirms project's viability. It is the first major and critical yard stick of importance for decision making.

Though this analysis is usually done for major investment proposals/assignments with long gestation schedules, it is desirable that this exercise be kept in mind while handling other important assignments too. In fact, let it be your routine when assigned with the responsibility of executing projects irrespective of their size and financial outlay.

The team chosen for implementation of such a project is expected to evaluate the analysis's details personally to understand the implementation schedules and also be aware of and be satisfied with the inputs listed in the report.

The SWOT analysis thus done would help in taking a calibrated view devoid of emotions. A step in haste any time may result in error of judgment. Be judicious; evaluate options before coming to a conclusion. The quality time spent at the stage of analysis shall bring up surprises later; surprises of sweet success, of the sense of accomplishment and achievement. In other words, a sound foundation shall be laid which will enable the proposed venture, project or option to grow smoothly.

Strengths mean availability of qualified and experienced manpower, detailed project report or profile of the job, adequate physical resources and other inputs essential for executing the project. It also includes project manager's exclusive personal expertise, dominance in similar projects earlier and his/her experience of having executed similar projects successfully within the allotted time frame and resources earlier.

Weaknesses would mean insufficient/incomplete details of the project profile, lack of adequate financial resources, lack of your personal experience of handling such a project earlier, non-availability of qualified personnel of appropriate talent and likely delays, if any, in availability of physical inputs.

Opportunities mean your advantageous position of facing no competition from elsewhere or your rich proven experience for similar projects and/or your exclusive qualification necessary vis-à-vis others.

Threats can be in the form of fierce competition, difficult logistics, adverse law and order issues or your inability to manage resources in time.

Inspiring Leadership Qualities

What else matters the most apart from the satisfying SWOT analysis? It is the inspiring leadership qualities that would be required the most for success of a venture.

It is said first impression is the last impression. Therefore, it is important for a leader to be able to inspire his men in the first interaction itself about his/her competence to handle the project effectively. Convey that we can and will perform well but together only. The quality of your earlier solo great performance doesn't inspire and do not brag about it at any stage with the team. Your ability to communicate effectively, confidently and persuasively with the team in the first interaction itself is a critical landmark. Be firm but polite in your interaction. Your communication style has to be such which removes the barriers of hesitation in their minds and invokes their response without any inhibition. Unless the communication channel in the team is well established, good performance and happy outcome remains elusive.

Leading by example, utilizing skillfully the collective potential of the team, mystically inspiring the top echelon of the group to build and rest not till the goal is achieved is the core material expected of an inspiring leader. It buttresses your hunger to be more ambitious and provides the satisfaction of being a successful leader and not just another individual.

Persuasively convince and demonstrate to the team that the success knows no bounds. The more you taste it and achieve it, the more demanding it turns out to be. It demands core competence and ability of committed individuals who trust and believe in themselves and are gifted with abilities to handle the task effectively in thick and thin of circumstances.

CHAPTER 4

NO SPACE FOR FANFARE IN WORK LIFE

Dream Big To Achieve Big

"Dream is the wife who must talk; sleep is the husband who silently suffers."

Rabindranath Tagore

The size and nature of achievement you are expecting/ visualizing is always directly proportional to the size and nature of the dream you have in mind. Therefore, dream big to achieve big to add big and rich value to life. Push yourself hard. This will force you to ramp up and match your efforts with the big dreams to be able to secure them.

I believe; healthy dreams, when achieved, glow and their shine is reflected in your eyes and your face. A unique glister and charm get added to your persona as a whole. An amiable personality is the reward you can expect on successful fulfillment of your dreams provided they are clean and good for the society.

Well, the dreams, big or normal, push us to a life of challenges. The difference is that while big ones compel us to explore harder and find out bigger options, the normal ones permit us to take it rather easy. Healthy and positive dreams widen our vision and broaden our perspective. They force us to sharpen our skills and strengthen our will to climb up and attempt to fulfill the dream regardless of obstacles, if any. Remember, there has to be no looking back. Take a vow and relax not till you are successful in achieving what you dreamt.

Big and honestly true dreams give rise to far-sightedness and missionary zeal and push for execution of the designated plans. A sense of restless attitude and positive determination to succeed oozes out of the mind then. Do not relax and do not relent till you succeed in your mission and are able to deliver to your own satisfaction and achieve really big.

Dreams excite and induce us to look for life's motto. Dreamers are visionaries. They think of future, work out strategies for growth and welfare of common good.

A question can be; why dream at all and why not be satisfied with life as it unfolds on its own? Yes, if you do not feel excited about your future. Remember: no dreams and normal life means only status-quo. No ambitions, no creativity, no urge to move up the ladder and be noticed and appreciated as a performer means a meaningless life. If human beings were to remain in-active and lethargic not believing in creativity and contributing nothing to enrich the heritage, that would be the saddest day for humanity. Let's remember; the faculty to dream has been bestowed on human beings only. It is expected of us to make maximum use of this innovative gift and visualize what should be done to enrich life.

Dream big to add big value to life. This will force you to ramp up and match your efforts with the big dreams you have in mind. The size and nature of dream(s) is directly proportional to the achievement(s) you are expecting/visualizing.

There are umpteen theories about the type of dreams and how and which type signifies what but, in my view, the first obligation we the human society has is to thank Him for the benevolence of capability to dream. (Any analytical study about types of dreams and their impact is not the talking point here.)If there were no dreams, there would be no ambitions, no creative thinking, no growth and human beings would be face to face with dullness as was the case in primitive periods. If people didn't dream, there would have been no research, no discoveries, no inventions, no industry, no creativity, no innovative surprises and absolute darkness/ignorance would be ruling our planet. Therefore, it is important that we all dream, dream big to be able to chase that elusive dream of un-paralleled success. But daydreaming, as they call it be better avoided as it is always a source of misery and pain.

Let's be futuristic, celebrate the long list of boons which have been possible thanks to big dreams of visionaries, great scientists, thinkers, reformers, professionals and persons endowed with missionary zeal. The growth this planet has witnessed since the times of Adam & Eve is before us. Today man is the master of skies, has conquered the space and Himalayan heights, thanks only to big dreams of scientists, engineers, technologists and other experts. The green revolution in agricultural technology has made it possible to feed the ever increasing population all around.

And, above all, the charm is that humans have not stopped dreaming, rather it is gaining strength and surprises will continue to flow as long as there is life on this planet.

Continue Chasing Dreams

The real tough journey begins after the first step on the ladder of success. Leisure, comforts and easy times disappear the moment one keeps his/her first foot forward in the hallowed territory of dreams and ambitions. Beware: you have entered the dream-land of your own creation and choice. Persist and enjoy every move that you make in this sacred territory otherwise the dream will turn into a nightmare depriving you of the peace of mind. Remember, it was a well-planned and thought out effort that made it possible for you to enter the exclusive territory of dreams. Keep looking ahead for going back is out of reach. Your every move has to be fast forward for there is no other choice, even sideway movements are prohibited. Get quickly reconciled to the changed environment, happily accept it and see it makes your journey smooth and hassle free. And be sure: hereafter the struggles that you make in your endeavors will be a pleasure rather than a burden.

Do not be in undue hurry. Remember, the outputs multiply when the inputs flow out of a relaxed attitude and earnest commitment.

Challenging Attitude: An Absolute Necessity

Challenges abound in the work life of those who dream of being recognized as star performers. Challenges take over the reins and catch hold of their imagination and creative faculties. One gets the message, "Now is the time for being innovative and original."Be aware of the broad contours of the challenge including its critical components. Work out detailed action plans, prepare blue-prints of activities to be undertaken, identify the options and inputs available, muster resources (financial and physical both) necessary for accomplishing the task and get going with your team or alone, as may be necessary." For nothing else matters other than meeting the challenges successfully.

A dreamer who gets a challenging assignment in critical functional area of the Company or Office is lucky but luckier is the one who secures such an assignment only after making serious efforts to get in. This is indicative of one's pro-active hold on ambitions with an ultimate aim of a successful career. For such persons, the challenge gets magnified and makes the seeker's task more difficult. You are subject to envy if you succeed but you are subject to ridicule if you fail. The brave souls don't get disheartened just for the fear of a possible failure. Their self-confidence gives them energy, courage and wisdom to overcome obstacles, if any. The opposite of this is true in the case of those who shirk responsibility and dare not to enter the river for fear of getting drowned.

The Hindi proverb, *"Jin khojya tin paya gehre paani baith"* means you are able to achieve only after getting to the root of the problem/task. The seekers achieve success only after scanning the depth and substance of the subject matter before them.

My mother used to tell, *"Gudri ke lall chhupaye nahin chhupte."* This means, the diamonds gleam even when put in a sack. Be a star performer and earn the sobriquet of a mad dreamer.

Self-Confidence; a Big Propeller

Self-confidence means being sure of one's capability/ competence of facing ups and downs of life and challenges as if in routine. No special efforts need be put in every time a challenge appears. Be always ready to face life and its challenges as they unfold. Self-confidence gets strengthened and gets built up by repeated acts of steady behavior in the face of difficult situations. Lack of self-confidence means loss of faith in one's attitudinal strength.

Always persist zealously and honestly with your efforts. Do not bother about delays, if any, in appreciation coming your way. Success speaks on its own. One only has to be stead-fast and ready to face obstacles and hindrances on the path with self-confidence. Such is the magic of self-confidence that gradually one starts believing in the inevitability of success in life. Entertain no doubts. It is a realistic approach.

Another important aspect self-confidence brings up is recognition and respect for you in your life. No matter where you are, your ability and competence are noticed always and it ensures a place of respect for you. Yes, you may become an eye-sore in the eyes of the lazy and non-performers. Just ignore all this and be steadfast in your resolve. Be careful and do not brag about your happiness in front of such people. Must avoid coming into conflict with them. You may be into trouble at their hands if you antagonize them. Beware; you are an honest fellow busy in delivering your best in the assignments before you. Keep it up as usual not caring to listen to rumors and whispers of despair.

Love Thy Profession

Can success and growth happen if one is not enthusiastic about his/her profession? No, life remains more or less static, unless one's mind is in sync with his/her profession. For such a person, compelling urge and stimulus which are so essential for great performance do not occur. The underlying sense of regret or unhappiness in mind remains active and thus one is unable to deliver his/her best. It reminds me of my younger son, Ashish. Right from is school days, he was dreaming of being a great physician. He believed; a good doctor enables one to be of service to suffering humanity. However, when reminded of very low wages as a Junior Resident Doctor compared to other professions, his response was really heart-warming. I don't care. I love my profession which enables me to serve the humanity.

Follow the maxim, 'Love thy profession and your job' for much sought after peace of mind. Job satisfaction is the foundation out of which peace of mind, a calm and creative attitude gush out. Job satisfaction is the best reward one can hope to earn.

Remember the universally applauded saying, 'yeh dil mange more' and see your job is easy and enjoyable. Do not sit back to bask in the glory of success. Keep pushing to move ahead still higher and higher. The journey may appear to be tough initially but do not worry, it shall become your routine. Be pro-active always. Never bother about hindrances, if any, for they are more imaginary than real. It is said, no barrier is too big when one is determined to achieve big.

CHAPTER 5

HANDLING MAJOR PROJECTS

For successful and timely execution of major projects, Mission Mode style is the right approach. Mission mode means executing the project with a missionary zeal by a group of committed individuals who believe the execution of the project before them is an important mission. This style of decision making is a well recognized approach for the execution of big projects and challenging assignments: assignments/projects having long gestation periods and critical long term implications. Such projects call for non-reversible determination to complete the assignment within the prescribed parameters; financial as well as the time frame.

For the execution of such projects, normally a team of professionals of different professions/skills is selected. The real benefit of this mode is that it enables quick decision making by the composite team of professionals of different disciplines in accordance with Mission's charter. Not only that, the actual implementation is also rendered easy thanks to absence of procedural wrangles and pricks.

Monitoring of the progress of implementation of various segments by the respective team leaders of the mission leads to effective controls and avoiding slippages etc.

For the Mission to be able to meet its avowed objectives, the authorities at the helm have to select and make available to the Mission the persons of real missionary zeal. Just calling it a Mission is not enough by itself. The fact is that unless the execution is in the hands of crusaders, there are strong possibilities of the Mission being not successful or facing financial and/or time over-runs.

And top of all; the choice of Head of the Mission would decide the fate of the Mission. He/she has to be an inspiring leader apart from being a crusader. Therefore, the choice of lead persons in the group must be the result of due diligence about their abilities and commitment to the objects of the Mission. I re-affirm from my personal experience that a challenge is half met when real crusaders take charge of a project.

Cohesiveness and oneness of the team are major planks for the success of the Mission. This mode demands that the team members give best of their creative ability and competence so that at the end of the day the team is proud of having successfully completed the project in time and within the resources allocated for the project.

Major projects have far reaching implications for achievement of targets and it is always important to ensure that the project is completed within the allotted resources and the prescribed time limit. Authorities/ Seniors hate time and cost over-runs for obvious reasons.

Mission Mode in Practice

I do have to my credit a memorable rich experience of successful completion of a major computerization project in Bokaro Steel Limited. Well before the production of finished rolled products was to start, a need was felt for "An Integrated computerized System of Production Planning, Order Processing, Shipment and Invoicing". It involved setting up a team of personnel of EDP dept. Production Planning, Quality Control, Shipping, Traffic Dept., and Accounts Dept. Not getting into the background and details of this concept, I would emphasize here that the need for introducing such a massive computerized system required a sincere team effort. Cohesiveness of the multi-disciplinary team was the key element for successful completion of the Mission. Accounts Dept. though at the end of the stream, was the major end-user of the project: preparation of computerized invoices, (about four hundred per day) to be done within twenty four hours of the shipment of the goods and preparation of various outputs necessary for computerization of detailed sales accounts thereof.

Being the major beneficiary and important end user, I played an important role in project's successful completion. I am proud I gave in my best along with other members. I still remember with awe and gratitude the names of leading members of the team and their zealous commitment to the objects/aim of the project. We were lucky in one more sense. Our inspiring seniors were equally committed and enthusiastic about the successful completion of the project. They would intervene and take up the issue in their own hands and resolve the differences.

It was a first unique computerization project attempted in mid seventies when no packages were available and the programming team was to design the project on their own with the help of Cobol etc. It was a marathon attempt successfully completed in an enthusiastic manner.

The project called for integrated processing of orders, production planning, quality control, shipment and dispatch of the loaded railway wagons, handing over of dispatch advices to Accounts to enable preparation of invoices within twenty four hours of the shipment. A first of its kind: the invoice preparation group of accounts section was working in three shifts of eight hours each. The composite team did face hiccups but gradually the entire process settled down as a routine.

It is said; a task well begun is half done. A well planned concept, cooperative effort, clear objective, mutually complete understanding between the team members and inspiring seniors make the journey smooth and truly lead to achieving the goal.

A Peep into Our Mission's Journey

Sincere commitment to the job was a big morale-booster for us. And we continued with our efforts fully satisfied.

But, in the process, all of us had become addicts and workaholics to the core. Nothing could under-mine either our enthusiasm or commitment to the project. That all this happened in Govt. sector would appear to be unbelievable. I know, even in Private sector, such a high level of motivation, team-work, camaraderie and sincere commitment is rare.

The bare fact is that the team loved its job without which such a challenging assignment couldn't have achieved its glorious closure. Each one of us believed; the team was on a mission. Project's successful completion was what really mattered. It was a team effort in true sense of the word. Believe me, in my chequered career of about four decades I never faced such a subtle enthusiasm again in a group. None of us ever felt the project was mighty difficult. We will do it and in time was our target. While designing and finalizing the contours of soft-ware and computer files etc. we would be silently busy. A peep into our office room would suggest we were sitting idle; no-body talking, just sitting and smoking and by implication wasting time. But, as is natural in such groups, we, in fact, would be busy scratching our brains to find an answer to an apparently mundane question(s). Even the exchanges in the group would apparently be suggestive of a drift. The old-time famous tale of opium-addicts in huddle would appear to be unfolding itself in the group. Innovation and out-of-box thinking was the forte of the tam. As a user of the system, I would explain broad contours of our existing manual working and also spell out my requirements of computerized out-puts leaving it to the EDP fellows to design the composite computerized system.

Such heartening and smoothening memories are ensconced deep somewhere in my inner-self. It is ecstatic to recall them and be deeply happy as if you are back to the same era and are living them once again and enjoying the thrill.

The Moral; A team of motivated individuals led by a competent and inspiring leader can deliver what may appear to be daunting rather near-impossible task. Give the team a clear mandate and functional autonomy; provide whole-some support and periodic doses of encouragement. Monitor but do not interfere, provide the team with resources and functional help as needed. Have patience and faith: amazing results would surprise you.

CHAPTER 6

BINDING THREADS IN WORK LIFE

Being Ambitious

There is nothing wrong in being ambitious and to aspire for scaling greater heights in life. In fact, this is the music of life; soothing and charming. The urge to be ambitious is God's Gift to the chosen ones. It doesn't come so easily to all. It may be hereditary, may have something to do with one's inner urges or it could be a product of deep influence of the stories of success of past heroes learnt/ picked up in the journey of life, or a combination of some of them. Ambitions for being realized demand creativity, innovative approach, out-of-the box thinking, patience to listen with open mind the divergent views, ability to do unbiased analysis, capacity/hunger to tread unchartered territories skillfully and above all a never tiring attitude.

It is eminently true that ambition is a superlative virtue. It helps create wealth not only for the individual himself/herself but also creates avenues of employment for scores of others. It also helps provide products/services for common good.

Ambition produces energy so vital for accomplishing a task. Harness it carefully and see it multiplies itself to be available for the next task.

Ambition by itself does not lead to achievements. Ambition is just a propeller. It is a switch that ignites the fire and stimulates hunger for action. The critical requirement for ambition to be a success story is a clear vision of what an individual aims to achieve. One must be aware of one's strengths, weaknesses and level of conviction one is gifted with. Ask, "Do I have the potential or some basic skills and training upon which I can build a mansion of my ideas? Am I aware how the perceived ideas can be achieved; what inputs and skills are essential for pushing ahead with the ideas? Do I already have those inputs and skills or have to manage to acquire them? If so, find out how to acquire them?

Blind and blank ambition without an aim and a clear vision is the very negation of capability to accomplish and would result in frustration. It could turn out to be a feeling of failure, of guilt and of self-deception. On the other hand, over-ambitious and utopian ideas lead nowhere.

Ambitious Souls; the Flag Bearers

An ambitious mind never takes a pause. Each success motivates such persons to seek more and more. A discerning mind and eyes feel, "Why settle for less when opportunities do keep un-folding one after the other for the seekers?" A pertinent incident which was narrated by one of my friends truly highlights the gut feelings of an ambitious mind. My friend's son-in-law, a young officer in the Indian Army happened to visit New York, sometimes in 1980s, on a short vacation. On return to India, this young officer was restless and showing signs of un-easiness. When asked to explain his dilemma, this man stated, "I saw Dollars lying scattered all over the place. Those who can see them will be blessed when they jump in with determination and make serious moves for getting a pie thereof. What a fantastic opportunity is there?" Obviously, this young officer had the vision, an insight to see beyond what meets the eyes. And few months later, I got the news that this visionary had quit his secure job in the Army and had joined his friend in New York as a partner. Later on, I came to know; this gentleman started, on his own, the business of importing hand-made and embroidered fancy fabrics etc and never looked back.

The moral of this story: have a vision of a compelling urge to seek more and more from yourself. Pick up a lesson or two from the tales of growth of others. Visualize a dream of a similar growth for yourself. Scratch your head, find out what you should do to accomplish and make the dream a reality. Involve yourself seriously in finding out an option or two to achieve your dreams. Only those become happy who wake up and put in serious efforts to fulfill the ambitions nursed in their minds.

In practice, however, it all depends on how you view the purpose of life: hard-working and committed to achieving more or just satisfied with a modest growth and feeling satisfied in a simple cozy job. Many factors, some positive and some negative come across before us, impact our mind and influence our faculties. Our ability to look for and to find out what best suits our psych shapes and firms up our goals.

The recent success stories of Start-Ups reveal what committed youngsters can achieve given the push and support by the authorities. Looking to the success stories of these professionals, I get a sense of sort of envy: envy of not getting the free environment of support in our times. For us, a secure govt. job was the ultimate success story. Entrepreneurship was a far cry for the middle class then.

The Flip Side of Being Over-ambitious

Success achieved after fulfilling one's ambitions is welcome but beware it also has some lurking pitfalls associated with it. Unscrupulous ambitions and success are always surrounded by arrogance, misdemeanor, and greed. These attributes are not only dangerous and highly harmful but are also quite eager to unleash their venom if one is not careful and vigilant. Arrogance shoots up from no-where just after the first signs of success, is followed by the tendency to be intolerant followed by the big brother, greed. While a discerning ambitious person may be well-aware of not letting the success, arrogance, ill behavior and greed spoil him/her. Some others, nay the majority gets swayed by the success and thus they enter into a phase of arrogant behavior and greed.

Arrogance leads to high handedness and ill behavior in general. Greed knows no limits. The more you succeed and accumulate huge wealth etc. the more you become hungry for it and start indulging in all sorts of malpractices. Greed is like a river in flood with its gushing waters destroying what comes in its way; breaching the embankments, uprooting trees, destroying crops, killing animals/human beings, entering the habitations and leave behind a trail of misery, destruction and countless problems of rehabilitation of the affected people and a trail of epidemics. Similarly, unfettered ambition leads to destruction of values, provides stimulus to use of unfair means like crony capitalism, evasion of duties and taxes, wide-spread corruption bringing untold miseries for vast population and degradation of moral fabric.

The unscrupulous ambition makes one believe he is always right, has superior place in society making him immune to scrutiny and that he is not doing any wrong. Such people live in an illusionary world of make-believe of their own creation and face the consequences sooner or later.

Mahatma Gandhi's vision of being a trustee of the empire is the real answer. It brings about contentment (Trupti in Hindi) which is most sacrosanct idiom of a really blissful and satisfied life. Nothing more remains to be achieved in materialistic domain then. Give back a reasonable share of your affluence to the institutions busy in welfare and up-lift of the poor. Repay your debt to society at large in whatever focused manner you deem right. Be righteous and grateful to all those who prompted you to push ahead.

Self Centered Attitude; Self-defeating

Self-centered means being egocentric and ego means self-esteem, conceit. Human beings are very intelligent, have been gifted with brains. It is expected that they make use of this boon for taking a balanced and enlightened view of life or a given situation as such before making a call. Making a positive and objective use of this capability is what a learned individual is expected to do. However, it is also true that most of the human beings are prone to ignoring this benign call. They dwell just within self only ignoring the bigger picture; the picture of being socially responsible and responsive. Such persons are the most self-centered creatures on the earth. For such persons nothing else, except self, matters. Their short-sighted vision blocks an honest and enlightened approach in life. For them, every move that serves their narrow self-interest is justified irrespective of its negative and harmful impact for others or society at large. Self is supreme and its interests, whether justified or not, are supreme and must always be taken care-of. If this tendency is not checked and controlled in time, it gives rise to a tendency of tolerance-less pursuit of unscrupulous self-interest. This is followed by greed and its concomitant siblings of dishonesty and degradation of basic values.

It is nobody's case that pursuing self-interest is bad in itself. This universe would not sustain if there was no self-interest. It is the most powerful tool and motivation for growth and development. Being selfish is neither unnatural nor retrograde. It means taking care of one's own interests but not at the cost of or exclusion of others' and society's good.

Being self-centered narrows one's vision and sharpens focus on pettiness in behavior. It is then that one cannot visualize anything other than satisfying blindly one's personal ambitions only. For a self-centered individual, protecting self-interest justifies any or all actions; whether bad and reprehensible or even if such thinking severely impacts others' interests. The political classes of the day are the most visible example. Most of them do not blink an eye even when entire community's or even country's interests are at stake.

A question arises whether blind pursuit of self-interest leads to satisfaction and happiness? No, such an attitude often pricks and imbalances one's general approach to life. The ultimate outcome can be a skirmish in one's thought process and a disturbed mind.

When is being Proud Justified?

Being proud of one's great performance and achievements in life is the music one must aspire to listen. It is a great feeling. It rejuvenates and builds up self confidence.

Strive, work hard and deliver against odds even and only then feel proud. However, one has to take care to ensure that the pride is not misplaced and doesn't lead to perfunctory approach. I think the context and accompanying circumstances would determine whether the pride is realistic, genuine and justifiable. If not, it may result in a serious negative attribute of which one should be wary. Even when the achievement is genuine and hard-earned, neither glamorize it nor flaunt it indiscriminately. If done, it is sure to lead to arrogance. And arrogance in any form or of any hue is nothing but the very negation of the values. Let's understand, self-pride is a positive attribute when it is accompanied by humbleness, has its genesis in achievements of positive nature like any recognition and awards.

The sense of being proud of success is an elixir: sweet and charming. It produces energy in abundance and propels us to give our more and more in this direction. It pushes us and gives a meaningful sense of direction to our initiatives. We feel motivated to excel and make attempts to beat our own past accomplishment.

Summing up; be positive, humble and focused. Keep pushing forward. Whatever be the odds, forget the phrase, 'I am tired.' Success follows those who believe in self and genuine hard work. Look to the Almighty when at cross-roads. Do not lament or complain. Take a pause and introspect to know what went wrong, what is the way out. Prayers and sincere hard work combined together never fail. There may be some temporary set-back but remember: the genuine and honest efforts ultimately throw up sweet results. Have faith; God is humanity's hope and last Resort.

When is being Proud Negative?

Being proud is negative when it is shallow, when it is rootless, when it is not based on actual performance. Self pride based on self-assumed success which is not corroborated by facts is nothing but just arrogance. Also, when one starts showing pride on the assumption of one's high pedigree, it is nothing but sheer arrogance. Such an attitude also leads to high handedness in one's dealings with others. A tendency of self assumed righteousness in one's conduct becomes yet another off=shoot of such an attitude. The result could be isolation in society leading to others avoiding such a person with obvious consequence. An attitude of self-assumed high place and high status in society is a negative pride. Believing that the wealth I possess is my pride is a fallacy. Should one take pride in possessing huge wealth? No, unless one possesses a philanthropic attitude and supplement it with actual performance. Otherwise, it is just arrogance. Some people might be ok in their minds with their manipulative style and some other similar negatives. It's nothing but a negative pride.

Some people believe being proud is itself the negation of virtues and is the antidote to being humble. In their opinion, being proud is poisonous, is always a negative attribute and therefore, not desirable. I think, feeling happy and satisfied with self is a morale booster but flaunting it indiscriminately is not. What is so bad about being proud of one's achievements if they are in positive domain, are genuine supported by actual facts and are laudable? I believe; being justly proud stimulates. Only, a proud person can dream big for he/she is full of enthusiasm to do more and is keen to touch/conquer the new peaks.

Success leads to pride and widens the horizon. Of course, it is important to be careful lest the pride takes the form of boorish vanity. Getting afflicted with vanity means the start of downward journey.

CHAPTER 7

GROWTH: A UNIVERSAL URGE

"We are in this world not to be happy but to grow."

Dr. Sarvapalli Radhakrishnan

Growth means an attitude of development, an idea and a vision of progress and happiness. It's a beginning in mind of the process of thinking for development. It is a cherished dream of aspiring individuals. Growth is life and is an important segment of human psych. On the contrary, no urge for growth means believing in status-quo and what can be more disgusting than such an attitude. This also leads to lack of will to aspire for recognition and securing for self an enviable identity in society. It is nothing but an anti-dote to human psych. Let's understand; the idea of growth is inherent in human psych. It has to be dug out of slumber if at all necessary. Thereafter, this urge pushes the individual to visualize and look for various options of concrete action plans followed by a resolve to succeed, come what may. For committed individuals, there is no going back then.

Creativity: Mankind's Magna-Charta of Growth

Creativity means having the power or ability to create things. Being creative means possessing the skills to show imagination and originality. It is commonly believed that all human beings are ambitious and are born with creative faculties of learning, conceptualizing and giving a unique shape of their liking to their idea(s) of life and growth. This significant thought lies at the bottom of urge in mind to be original and comprehensively imaginative.

Strain your creative faculties and let them loose in the arena of your exclusive domain of wishful thoughts. Such an exercise once initiated is sure to throw up creative and original ideas of long lasting significance. Blessed are those who get this realization as the only option for a healthy growth in life.

Be creative and focused to see wide vistas of thought-provoking and fulfilling ideas opening up before you. Then follow the meaningful and healthy ambitions which build up pressure and push the seekers to look for options thought to be essential and appropriate for growth. Nothing can stop such individuals thereafter. They get earnestly busy in firming up their implementation plans and right options of growth. Thereafter, begins the journey of pushing ahead determinedly and relentlessly till success is achieved.

On the other hand, shallow and whimsical thoughts lead nowhere. They create a world of make-believe especially for those who believe in miracles and indulge in day-dreaming. In my opinion, such persons build up misfortunes for themselves and keep regretting for the rest of their life. The famous story of Sheikh Chilli's ambition to be a rich person one day with the help of an egg only is a pointer to the plight of those who do not believe in creative action and indulge in wishful thinking only. The path of glorious achievements demands: be creative, shun the ideas of miracles, act and do not rest until success is achieved.

Lord Krishna says, *"Act you must sincerely hard with honesty of purpose and leave the outcome to ME."*

Education & Training: the Vital Components for Growth

May be you do not possess adequate resources to sustain life as expected by you. Be positive and do not rest until you find out ways to make efficient use of whatever avenues/resources are available. In the beginning when you do not have the comfort of sufficient material resources, concentrate on moderate aims but do not overlook the most critical ingredient for success; proper education and training. Education widens horizon, clears the cobwebs of misconceptions, prejudices and helps create positive mood. It banishes the thoughts of bad luck and generates positive thinking. Hundreds of thousands, world-wide, acquired education despite misery or lack of adequate facilities. Tales abound of determined minds doing manual labor during the day and studying during night under the street lamp-posts. Great success, world-wide recognition and applause came their way in the end. Inspire yourself from their stories and pick up a lesson or two from the glowing lead left behind by such worthy elders. It is said, 'God helps those who help themselves.' Believe sincerely in this edict. One loses self pride and the will to grow the moment one seeks gratuitous help.

Pamper and inflate your ego with focus on positive traits, buttress it with the thought of putting in your best. Entertain no false ideas about your strengths. False notions about own capabilities lead to a down-ward journey no sooner then you have embarked on it. Be a real and hard task master for self. Be vigilant and expect more from self. Look around and identify those who made it big in life and who inspire you. Do not relax until you see some tangible first rays of hope. Persist with efforts as planned. Keep pushing and be motivated by the stories of your inspirers' great achievements. Pick up from the leads provided by such worthy elders who left behind shining examples of success despite lack of proper resources.

Positive Thinking: A Stimulus for Growth

Positive thinking means being positive in approach and not allowing negative thoughts to enter your thought process. One should see events as they unfold in a positive manner and discard negative ideas if any unfolding in mind. Apply your unbiased mind on the issue to look at the facts. Believe in self, have confidence in your ability to separate chaff from the grains. The facts thus revealed will help in finding out the correct position. Avoid being misled by whims and prejudices of others. Have confidence in your ability to judge things rationally. Such an approach cajoles and calls for being aware of one's strengths and weaknesses. With this knowledge at your command, be single-mindedly active and push ahead hard in the right direction. You will see vast opportunities unfolding before you. Sustain this awareness and build up total faith in self. Gradually, it leads to a stimulus of choice for pushing ahead in all spheres of life. This, in my opinion, is called positive thinking.

Purpose of Life

"Your purpose in life is to find your purpose and give your whole heart and soul to it."

Gautam Budha

The phrase tells that each individual has to dwell deep in mind to determine and find out his/her object/aim in life. It conveys that one ought to know what he/she expects from self and what the objective/purpose of life is for him/her. Is it just to add to comforts and create wealth or you think life is a much bigger phenomenon? Making life comfortable etc. is said to be a normal expectation and a vast majority yearns to make it happen. There is nothing wrong about it. However, for conscientious individuals, life underscores and carries much bigger and lofty aims; undertaking to help the needy, the poor, rendering community service in different forms, doing acts for social good, coming to the rescue of persons suffering from natural calamities and epidemics etc. There are other endless options for rendering help in similar other situations and coming forward for help in community development programs. Yet; for some individuals, trying to connect with HIM through penance, meditation and prayers can be the purpose of life.

On the other hand, aimless existence is a curse and points to an existence like animals. *"Subah hoti hai, sham hoti hai, zindagi bus youn hi tamam hoti hai"*. Days and nights come and go and life exists without any purpose. Is it what nature expects from a human being who has been blessed with brain? Or should we be busy just in satisfying our basic needs or hunger, providing clothing and similar other inconsequential urges? The way out is to assert, cajole self out of slumber and get going in pursuit of higher goals.

Challenges Resilience Faces

Life is not a bed of roses except for a few who are born with a silver spoon in their mouth. We all do face adverse situations in life. It is nothing unusual. In fact, it is a sort of challenge for those who believe in self.

Keep the long term interests in view and stay cool. Analyze the difficult situation. Let your creative faculties take charge. Be patient and self confident. Work on your capability to face the adversities as a challenge. Remind yourself, you are well-versed in meeting challenges. Be optimistic and get busy in finding a way out. Be reasonably patient, self-composed and peaceful. After finding the right option(s) for meeting the challenge, get busy in working on them. Make sure the outcome meets the objective of overcoming the challenges. Beware, ultimately the sincere efforts succeed.

I always did ignore pin-pricks and remained cool on the job, so to say. My steely resolve, 'Keep the feeling of discomfort away from mind and devote 100 % to job.' After all, performance only matters. Cribbing about sundry odd situations in work-place and blaming the circumstances is no remedy. Rather show good performance, as before. Your good performance is noticed and appreciated at appropriate times even in Organizations which one may feel un-comfortable with. That's the real challenge, real test of resilience in approach and delivery.

Being comfortable and showing great performance in conducive and convenient circumstances is no big play. It is the play-field of average and easy going souls. Ignore un-easy situations, continue to focus on performance and show you have faith in yourself to excel in odd and difficult situations also.'

Mutual adjustment: A step forward

Odds are part of life journey: whether personal or work life. Adjustment is the only option. The question is, should some odd incident or two of negative magnitude derail us or make us un-steady? Should we not trust our core values and belief in self? Should we feel helpless and not be able to ignore them? Should we not rely on our past incidents of resilience on such occasions? Should we just forget the passion with which great achievements were made during the course of our journey so far?

All these questions surfaced in my mind after I came across a disturbing incident which was nothing but the demonstration of the other person's ill-founded ego. It happened just in the beginning itself in an Organization which I had joined with great expectations. I was completely disturbed and for a while I thought I had taken a wrong decision of joining this organization. The other person was holding a high position in the Company. But I didn't lose my calm and kept silent. In fact, I had no other prudent option. Any rash decision was unthinkable given that the reasons which weighed with me before applying for the job in this Company were valid even now. And, in addition, I personally loved the place. I put together these and other positive and meaningful thoughts and calmed down my hurt ego. I decided to adjust well and put in serious efforts to regain my wits.

Leaving behind the odd incident, which had made me uncomfortable, I started being my normal self giving out my best as if nothing disheartening had happened. I was happy I did so. Recognition followed thereafter confirming my resolve of not getting destabilized with such pin-pricks.

PART III

CHAPTER 1

BRAIN STORMING JOURNEY

An Exercise for Self-Appraisal

What does self-appraisal mean? It means an honest attempt at knowing one-self fully well, the persona, the roots, strong and weak points and other attributes which are unique to an individual. This helps in being closer to self and a successful life being the aim. Such an appraisal helps in making attempts to overcome the weakness and celebrating one's good attributes.

Here are a few questions which may help in this endeavor.

- **Am I aware of the influence that my elders, teachers, school/college mates and other buddies in general left on me and in what manner did I use it to create my own unique personality?**

- **What is the meaning of true friendship for me? Do I believe that an honest approach in friendship is an endowment of values that help in steering life** happily? Am I selective in choosing friends? If so, how do I make a choice? Or, do I believe that friendship is an instinctive act which happens instantly and grows leisurely on its own?

- How do I see life: 'to be successful and happy or live life as it unfolds?'

- Life doesn't permit being just carefree. A meaningful life is possible only if one is aware of its true meaning and purpose. As such, one needs to be inquisitive, balanced and committed to pushing ahead on the right path and facing the challenges assiduously. Do I agree or have a different opinion?

- Am I aware of my strengths and weaknesses-physical as well as mental? Do I know how can I overcome my weakness and shortcomings?

- Do I care about details like dos and don'ts while working on my plans to succeed in my efforts?

- Am I in the habit of observing carefully and picking up lessons for my own benefit while reading some books and other literary pieces, watching some programs on TV, reading a newspaper/book/ magazine or listening to stories of great achievers? Do I believe that drawing lessons from the experiences of others is helpful in conducting the affairs of life?

- Do I feel, devoting some time in pursuing a creative hobby helps in soothing nerves and developing a balanced approach in life or I believe, being crazily busy in hard work only matters?

- Have I known that health is wealth and if so, am I careful in following this edict in my life?

- Do I think peace of mind is as important as money for a good living?

- Do I accept that the truth ultimately prevails and honesty is the best policy?

- Do I have an icon before me in whom I believe and whose life inspires me and motivates me? If yes, what lesson(s) did I learn from his/her journey?

- Does the reading of biographies of successful icons attract me in general and do I believe that it provides an opportunity for molding my approach for my own benefit in my own way?

- Am I aware of the legacy my elders left behind for the family? If yes, do the healthy values and traditions left behind by them inspire me? Do I follow some of them in my life? Did I try to find out if some diary or scribbled notes etc. were left behind by any of my ancestors? If yes, did I pick up some lessons after going through those documents?

- Do I feel it is essential to spend some time in the company of my living elders whose presence is a boon for the lucky souls and whose wise counsel is always freely available?

- **And above all, am I confident of myself? Am I aware of the intrinsic meaning of a successful life?**

- **Do the sufferings of the poor and down-trodden move me and do I feel like extending a helping hand to the needy? Being helpful and considerate is in my nature?**

- **Being in a comfortable position now, do I think, I should pay back to society for all what it gave to me? Philanthropy, being sensitive to the expectations of others and being compassionate in my conduct are closer to my heart?**

This exercise is intended to help you to be aware of your strengths and weaknesses enabling you to look ahead and seek options for change for betterment in life.

Do the self-appraisal, find out your answers and be happy if your response to most of the questions is positive.

CHAPTER 2

THE DEFINING STAGES IN LIFE

Childhood and Adolescence

The first stage comprises of childhood and adolescence, when the learning faculties and observation skills are put to use regularly without any big conscious effort. It is an opportunity for amassing inputs of great significance: the inputs that are capable of setting one's agenda for life. In this phase, a child's innocent mind is in receptive mode and is capable of picking up values and to add them to his/her knowledge base. The surroundings and environment in the house, individual's own attitude, bent of mind and ability to observe carefully what is happening around play an important role in its grooming. The inclination of careful observation is an opportunity for the child to pick up lessons from happenings around. In this phase of life, the mind is capable of differentiating between good and worthy of being retained and ignoring what is not.

The learning picked up at home, in school, in the neighborhood and in society as a whole, helps in developing the basic structure of values which get refined in due course and on which a final superstructure gets built up later. This entire process of learning keeps happening on its own without the individual consciously being aware of it. It is a formative and grooming stage. Lucky are those whose parents/other elders in the family are conscious of their role of a guide, helper, and enabler and spend quality time with their children. And still luckier are those who have their grandparents and other elders around. They have no constraints of time and are freely available for consultation. They feel naturally inclined by instinct of love to spend time with their grand children, share their experiences and provide guidance. Avail yourself of this golden opportunity, be benefitted by listening to their worldly wise anecdotes and enrich your life. Those who love them, respect them, feel free to open their mind and seek guidance are able to help themselves in difficult situations with confidence later in life.

It is a stage of accumulating healthy values and building up a castle of core-beliefs. Aided by formal learning in schools/colleges later, the structure thus created lays the foundation for a healthy super growth in adulthood.

Adulthood

The second stage begins with adulthood and when one enters the active work life. The basic inputs accumulated in the first stage come into full play now. With the help of a sound base of healthy values accumulated earlier, your journey now is capable of facing the ups and downs of life with confidence aided by your personal experiences in the practical field of work life. Those not so lucky have to struggle more and strain their nerves for building up a superstructure of values of their choice. It is the perseverance that is under focus and what follows is a cumulative output of their practical learning in life.

Adulthood is the stage of 'Karma' for all. Have faith and follow diligently Lord Krishna's edict in the Gita, 'Do your duty well and care not for the outcome.'

Make full use of the professional and technical knowledge gained in colleges/institutes and helped by worldly wisdom and your healthy value system, push ahead. Do not rest until you have made a success of your mission. Apply your open and receptive mind in the work place and the vast world around you. Care not for whispers of jealousy and back-biting. Perform well to your own satisfaction and deliver your best. Keep pushing determinedly. Nothing can stop you now. Glory will be all yours.

What has been stated above is the sum total of the personal experiences of my life. I was lucky and am sincerely grateful to my elders especially my mother in childhood and my worthy elder sister and brother-in-law in Dehra Dun during my formative years of 14-16 that made it possible for me to learn healthy lessons in childhood and adolescence. I owe it to them for whatever I achieved in life later as a grown up individual.

Old age

"Old as I am in age, I have no feeling that I have ceased to grow inwardly or that my growth will stop at the dissolution of the flesh."

Mahatma Gandhi

True. A person doesn't stop growing as one says good-bye to the formal phase of work-life. In fact, it is an enabler phase loaded with opportunities for achieving sublime and lofty aims of life. As one is nearing this phase of life, one starts getting the urge to plan in advance for pursuing the options which were lying dormant under the pressures of work-life. It all depends on the individual's circumstances and compulsions. But the fact remains that work life's varied pressures being off, one can choose to pursue other options of choice. The old age is no barrier for helping one-self in the manner one deems appropriate.

CHAPTER 3

MAKING LIFE EASY

A serious necessity for healthy growth and a fulfilling life is open, clean and alert mind to help create a strong pyramid of rich and healthy values.

Persevere to know self to be aware of your own propensities, good and bad both and your inclination of mind. Unless you know yourself fully well and are conscious of own traits, making a correct/desirable move in a given situation may not be possible. Introspect to zero in on the truth, when in two minds.

Learn from elders' meaningful practical tips/experiences and be free in seeking their advice when in difficulty. This reminds me of an old folk story. "During parleys on arrangements for marriage, the bride's people desired that the Barat should comprise of youngsters only. Obviously they had some funny tricks up their mind and believed that youngsters because of lack of worldly experience could easily be outwitted. Groom's grandpa realizing their trick, travelled with the marriage party (Barat) disguised as a young priest. During feast, the groom's fellow travelers (Baraties) were made to sit facing each other on the dining table with their arms tied straight with sticks. They were now face to face with each other: a serious dilemma, 'How to fold arms to be able to pick up food from the table?'At this, the so-called young priest started feeding the person sitting opposite to him with his unfolded arms. The rest of the Baraties followed suit. Thus, to the delight of every one, the marriage party (Barat) won the battle of wits, thanks to wise move of the elder amongst them.

Be polite, frank and open in your dealings with others. Keep smiling when interacting with others. Diplomacy better be left for diplomats and strategists.

Do not be a workaholic only. Take a periodical break, and relax in the company of those whom you love.

Do not fail in conveying to others your appreciation as a gesture of gratitude when you think it is due.

Strive to build up a sponge like base in brains for retaining and making use of relevant learning acquired in practical life-situations,

Have courage to own responsibility and offer apologies for failings, misdemeanor or other similar weaknesses. Find out own short comings and try to overcome them. Pinpointing instantly to others' misbehavior or display of rough attitude better be avoided. Just overlook it or wait for opportune moment to convey your unhappiness and a feeling of hurt.

Avoid confrontation and make the embarrassing situation lighter by focus on 'better forgive & forget' rather than carrying the burden of ill-will.

PART IV

CHAPTER 1

MISCELLANY

Post-retirement Life Scenario

It is a Challenge?

Even though the D-day is well known before hand, but when it comes, it turns out to be a wake-up call not only for the concerned individual but also for other members of the family. A sort of vacuum appears on the horizon. For many, it is a shock. There is no urgency to hurry up with the morning routine. The absence of pressure for hurrying up turns out to be a dilemma for many. For conscientious people, it is a challenge of sorts to put up a brave face in the family. The silent sense of sympathy if one comes across in the family or elsewhere becomes pinching. The fact is that brave souls or no brave souls, the unease lingers on for quite some time.

Well, can it also be said to be a feeling of relief? No, it is more like a wake-up call: reminding the individual of the change that has set in which demands re-orientation of priorities. One has to face the change with conviction/ confidence and adjust with it. After all it is there to stay.

Yes, it needs a determined mind to face the vacuum with confidence. Succumbing to the so-called vacuum and feeling disheartened is no remedy. Frankly speaking, it takes quite some time even for brave souls to get adjusted to the vacuum. But there is no option other than planning and coming up with a program of utilizing the available time in some constructive and meaningful activities of one's choice and liking.

A Mixed Challenge

This phase is a mixed challenge of sorts. The reduced monthly income is truly a challenge but there is also an expectation of other incoming silver linings too: freedom from the hectic life and enabling expectation of fresh start of a period of peaceful inning of choice: choice of starting with new options of choice for a healthy and meaningful spell in life.

How to manage household needs with reduced income and how to utilize gainfully and happily the free time available now? Both are a challenge of sorts until one resolves to face each one of them with confidence and determination.

Hold on: the scenario of reduced income (on the assumption that pension takes the place of salary) is not so grim as would seem to be unfolding. I believe: most of the individuals look before hand into the scenario of reduced income while in service and plan their strategies of augmenting income from other sources. This aspect is not beyond one's abilities to foresee it. Yes, managing finances can be planned before-hand. Also, it can be assumed that income of other grown up member(s) of the family is a possibility of some relief.

However, each retiree cannot be said to be in the same boat. For some, the financial crunch is the core reason for dissatisfaction for various reasons: pending education for some child or marriage of a ward or building a house etc. Advance planning could have helped but do not worry. Availability of bank loans for education or for building a shelter for the family are not constraints now. One needs to tighten the belt and manage such constraints within the resources at command.

The other concern, gainful utilization of the time available now is a serious poser. Whiling away time somehow is unthinkable. It must be avoided in the interest of being personally happy and satisfied with self in the first instance. An idle senior member of the family is not only a big drag for himself but also for other members especially the better-half. She would see you as a hindrance for smoothly managing her house-hold chorus. You must either be away from the scene for some time or be busy in some creative and purposeful activity. Therefore, the need of remaining busy and finding avenues for doing so should be addressed in time. It is said, "An idle mind is devil's workshop." To avoid such a stigma, one should pick up a purposeful creative activity to be happy and healthy. A definite idea and plan should be thought of beforehand. This is the only way out for beating the vacuum.

A prime reason for vacuum in most of the cases is non-pursuit of or lack of some creative hobby during active work-life itself. One may feel disheartened but giving up or repenting is no remedy. After all, there is no bar in making a beginning and start pursuing a creative line of choice now. Initially, there may be some internal resistance, a sort of mental barrier but a determined mind can overcome it. The choice of planned activity must be an act of well thought-out process. Give time to the churnings in mind and let your creative faculties do their job. Consult your better-half also and consider her suggestions with care and due attention. Such an outcome will be rewarding.

A Challenge and an Opportunity Both

To sum up: it all depends on how one takes this phase; just a challenge or a challenge and opportunity both. Yes, it is both, a challenge and an opportunity. Be optimistic and strain your thinking faculties to meet the challenges with determination. Revive and give impetus to your hobbies which lay dormant so far. It is an immense challenge to do it but never mind, your mature inquisitive mind is there to help you.

The remedy for meeting the financial challenge is within your competence. Face the challenge with equanimity/determination as you have been meeting the numerous other challenges all along your work-life and seize the opportunity of being your own master now. Handle the twin challenges with confidence. In fact; both are inter-linked. Your plans for future will take care of your anxieties of financial crunch also. It is quite possible. Your rich experience in living a life of challenges so far has conditioned your mind to coolly work out the options for a stable future. Take the burden off your mind and get going. Draw out plans, discuss them in your family especially your grown-up children, involve them, where possible and get going. Soon, you will accumulate lot of bouquets of satisfaction and happiness.

A new life-cycle of hopes and aspirations has begun now. Move along the cherished territory of peaceful and contented life.

Senior Citizens in Business

Our Holy Scriptures divide a human being's life into four stages of 25 years each and as per scriptures, Vanprastha, the third stage starts after fifty years of age when one is expected to start gradually withdrawing from active work-life. It is believed that elders in the family begin making way for the next generation so that the ultimate taking over by the next generation is without hiccups. However, in the present context of longevity of life span, gradual withdrawal can be delayed beyond 50 years of age. And the grown up member(s) can be given the responsibility of either another stream of business or upgrading the existing set up/structure. Computerization and adding other streams of business is also an option. In fact, your rich experience of many decades and energy of youngsters full of enthusiasm and determination is an asset for growth of business/industry.

Summing Up

A word of caution is desirable here; do not stretch yourself too much and do not enter the never-satisfying territory of over-ambition lest the whole process turns out to be a nightmare, severely painful and negative. A retired pension holder should not think of indulging in a maddening pursuit of accumulating wealth at the cost of loss of peace of mind and cherished values. Recall your singular achievements while in job and cherish the feeling of satisfaction all along.

Post retirement life is full of challenges and opportunities both. Look at your long-term goals and aims and plan accordingly for a composite life-after-job. Now, when the hustle bustle of hectic work-life is over, do have a look at and think of satisfying fine inner urges which lay suppressed under the carpet till now.

There are umpteen other ways of getting happily busy. Join either some existing NGO which has its focus on social welfare or create an NGO of your own. Yes, it would call for serious efforts at accomplishing it satisfactorily but, let's understand, it is not beyond a mature and experienced individual of your caliber. Make a small beginning to gain confidence. Associate with other like-minded persons and build up a team. Once in it with determination: co-operation and support will not be wanting. Human beings are intelligent social animals and value greatly an honest effort. Gradually, funds too will start flowing in. Let creativity have a chance to come to surface. Give it a free hand; you will be surprised with the results.

Similarly, those with some financial crunch can embark upon some business venture with the help of limited means at disposal. Plan it thoroughly well, consult some experienced individuals and draw out detailed plans/strategy. After all, the Banks and other lending institutions support such ventures if found to be viable and the promoter is able to convince them about plan's viability and revenue-earning potential.

After retirement, I too ventured into such an option, steered it well for six years and felt happy. I had very little capital of my own. To start with, my sleeping partner provided the funds but later the bank loan came to my rescue. This venture kept me busy like before: provided an opportunity to train young college-going students to acquire skills for a bright future in Sales & Marketing. The result- I was satisfied with my efforts and a large number of college-going young boys/girls found an opening of their choice.

Some Other Sublime Moves

Another serious avenue for getting happily busy is picking up some activity for one's inner-self. Post-retirement phase means less and less time for mundane activities. It is a time for working on something higher and sublime in addition to devoting attention to normal activities/

responsibilities. Be self-oriented and get busy, once again, but to achieve something bigger and praise worthy of personal choice.

It is expected that in due course the burden of handling worldly responsibilities passes on to the next generation. Get detached, as much and as quickly as possible, to enable smooth entry into the last phase; the stage for seeking total freedom, peace of mind and bliss. It doesn't mean leaving hearth and home and leaving for jungles. The concept of physical isolation (Sanyasa) doesn't make any sense for a person whose whole life has been action, action & action. Further, the revolution in communication technology has made it redundant now. Irrespective of where you are, introspect, look beyond normal to pursue the bigger goal and make attempts to leave behind a rich legacy of defining qualities a human being should aim at in life.

Another meaningful option can be pursuit of some creative activity like fine arts, book writing, other creative hobby (ies) and making efforts at trying to connect with inner-self. There are other options too. Figure out the option you cherish and think you have had a stint earlier but couldn't pursue it much being busy with job and other responsibilities. Take up the one which attracted you earlier.

It is in human nature that people over-estimate their performance arising either out of misplaced self-eulogizing euphoria or refuse to accept the true position, or do not believe in fair-play in their own dealings with others. Such persons suffer not because of others but because of their own limitations to accept the truth. In most of such cases, illusions of their superior capabilities or high pedigree are also the reasons for their grievances. Once you get into such a psychological cycle, it is difficult to come out of it making it a regular life-long habit.

To be happy and satisfied, cultivate the habit of working hard, accept willingly the need to perform sincerely well and try to see merit in 'honesty is a best policy.' Try to be balanced, open and fair in dealings with others. God willing, the journey will be smooth and the results highly encouraging.

In my childhood, I heard many times the popular saying, "Apni akkal, praya dhan, barra lagta hai" which means 'one's own wisdom and wealth of others' appears to be bigger. The truth behind this universal truth always remained with me and always warned me to never over-estimate myself in any sphere of life.